Winning the Math Homework Challenge

Winning the Math Homework Challenge

Insights for Parents to See Math Differently

Catheryne Draper

ROWMAN & LITTLEFIELD
Lanham • Boulder • New York • London

Published by Rowman & Littlefield
A wholly owned subsidiary of The Rowman & Littlefield Publishing Group, Inc.
4501 Forbes Boulevard, Suite 200, Lanham, Maryland 20706
www.rowman.com

Unit A, Whitacre Mews, 26–34 Stannary Street, London SE11 4AB

British Library Cataloguing in Publication Information Available

Library of Congress Cataloging-in-Publication Data   AUG 1 9 2017
Names: Draper, Catheryne.
Title: Winning the math homework challenge : insights for parents to see math differently/
    Catheryne Draper.
Description: Lanham : Rowman & Littlefield, [2017] | Includes bibliographical references.
Identifiers: LCCN 2016036996 (print) | LCCN 2016038990 (ebook) |
    ISBN 9781475829716 (cloth : alk. paper) | ISBN 9781475829754 (electronic)
Subjects: LCSH: Mathematics—Study and teaching. | Education—Parent
    participation. | Homework.
Classification: LCC QA135.6 .D73 2017 (print) | LCC QA135.6 (ebook) | DDC 510.71—dc23
LC record available at https://lccn.loc.gov/2016036996

Printed in the United States of America

Dedicated to all the students who taught me how to teach them.

Contents

Preface

Winning the Math Homework Challenge shares the stories of my students' reasoning, thinking, and sometimes misunderstandings about mathematics—stories that allowed me to see math differently, through their eyes. Most were visual learners who needed a visual explanation of the mathematics. The stories and illustrations in these pages are real. The names have been changed so that no one will feel the shame or embarrassment of being "found out." When I have shared these stories with parents and other students, their general response has been relief: relief that they are not alone and relief that it isn't their fault.

This book describes these students' experiences with mathematics. Like many teachers, I saved their materials, kept notes on their initial perceptions about the math concepts, recorded the activities that helped their learning *and* the activities that hindered learning, used learning-style assessments, read the psychological evaluations, and involved them in their own learning. I wanted them to teach me how to teach them.

My goal was to encourage them to take possession of, and responsibility for, their own learning. My venue was through their eyes and hands. Needless to say, I learned more about mathematics as I learned *how* to look at the math concepts through their eyes and then make the return trip through my own eyes. The process was completed only when the math concept was rerouted through the students' eyes, into their understanding, and then out again, while I watched them arrange and rearrange, listened to their explanations, or read their solutions.

Students started their turnaround from failure to success when the visual models and materials started making the math make sense. They could move the materials around, arrange, rearrange, and examine them from different perspectives. They could ask questions about the relationships *in the materials*. As students tried out new arrangements, a subtle yet effective transfer happened. Their aversion to the math transferred *from their core identity to the materials*. The math relationships were now in the materials, where they should have been all along. You will read more about this core identity confusion in the Math Avoider chapter.

Students also started to take responsibility for their learning, slowly and tentatively at first, by risking some opinions. They were beginning to feel like they may indeed *have some control* over their math learning! Everything rested on the phrasing of the question, mine to them and theirs to each other and back to me. It took awhile to instill a judgment-free zone. Some students took longer than others to risk an opinion or observation, but all of them eventually started their journey down their new path of experiences in mathematics.

As you read these stories, be prepared to get excited about understanding your own feelings and similar experiences through their words. Also, prepare to be challenged to understand their descriptions and explanations as seen through their eyes. My hope is that the stories in this book can help parents see mathematics through their children's eyes, both the clarity and the confusion.

Armed with this new sight, and therefore insight, parents will be able to talk differently with their children about math. These Math Avoiders, whether they are parents or children and whether they are math anxious, math annoyed, or math-distanced-neutral, might recognize themselves in these stories and feel more prepared to join the "Math Aficionados," those who actually like mathematics.

                                                                    C.D.

Foreword

A few years ago, as a mathematics education professor in the Department of Mathematical Sciences at the University of Montana and as president of the National Council of Teachers of Mathematics, it was important to stay in touch with how children were thinking and learning. To do this, I talked with a local teacher, and together we planned a unit on large numbers for her 23 heterogeneously grouped third graders. This class, with frequent parent participation, was accustomed to visitors, so, with the principal's blessing, we started the unit.

In a relatively short time, after asking about what large numbers they knew, I began to hear words like "a million," "a billion," "a trillion," "a zillion," and more like this, on up to and including "infinity." In the course of the class discussion, one relatively quiet student raised his hand and said, "I heard that you can compare infinities. Is that true?" I was both shocked and fascinated because I had not seen this notion until I was a senior undergraduate in mathematics and truly did not explore it until graduate school.

How could I respond in a meaningful way while not losing the other 22 students in the class? Instead of answering directly, I asked where he heard the idea, but he did not remember. We agreed to talk later, and when we did, his teacher and I were amazed at just how rapidly he had grasped a very complex notion and had such a sophisticated level of understanding. A later interview with the boy's parents (with little mathematics background) revealed that they were very conscientious about his learning but had never introduced the notion of infinity to him, and, like his teacher and myself, his parents were amazed that he was questioning mathematics at that level.

Looking back on that situation, I often wondered what the conversations might be like in the student's home of three children with well-educated parents. How might I have reacted to him on a daily basis had he been my child? His question and the depth with which he grasped a deep mathematical notion led me to believe that at some point in his later mathematics education, he might be lucky enough to have a collection of teachers who could probe and continually pose mathematical issues to him that would allow him to progress in a "non-normal" way even if in a normal classroom.

Or he could be unlucky enough to have a few teachers who would not be able to handle such inquisitiveness but might require that he work on mathematics concepts in a more traditional and pedestrian way. In the latter case, how might his parents encourage him and how might they approach his future teachers in a way that would not be threatening or disruptive, and in a way such that they would not appear to be helicopter parents trying to manage every aspect of his mathematical studies? I found that I did not have easy answers to these questions.

"Disengagement is too often reinforced in both overt and subtle ways by the attitudes and actions of adults who have influence with students."[1] To help alleviate those attitudes and actions, teachers are encouraged to "foster reinforcement of their efforts by families and other community members by maintaining dialogue aimed at the improvement of mathematics education."[2] This dialogue should include giving opportunities for families to ask questions, express concerns, and experience classroom activities, while learning about mathematics goals, students' learning, teaching, and programs. While these are wonderful ideals for teachers and parents, it must be recognized that such ideals sometimes get lost in the process of daily work of both teachers and parents. So, what can parents do?

Winning the Math Homework Challenge explores selected math topics and ideas so that families can be involved in their children's learning in positive ways. This exploration requires some family effort to learn the math and to learn how their child learns and thinks. They need to be able to recognize how their children are learning by studying the type of thinking that is being used. They need to ask themselves questions such as the following: Do their children need more visual clues, more verbal clues, or some other method of help as they explore and question? What types of intelligences are the children using? How could families help them make math more personal so that it becomes a part of the children's fabric as opposed to a patch?

Winning the Math Homework Challenge will help families begin to answer some of the questions while also helping them to begin to formulate their own questions both for their children and for the teachers of those children. A large message in the book is how to communicate with a child, a teacher, and a school system, if necessary, to help students learn mathematics from the early grades. A second large message is that a single family is not alone in this regard. This book might be used in a study group of families trying to sort out children's learning and thinking. In this way, the book is a valuable resource for families but also for teachers who need to know and recognize that the education of children is a joint effort and not a solitary task.

Johnny W. Lott

NOTES

1. National Council of Teachers of Mathematics, *Principles and Standards for School Mathematics*, 371.

2. National Council of Teachers of Mathematics, *Principles and Standards for School Mathematics*, 372.

Introduction

The information in these pages comes from students—their stories, their confusions, and their successes. The objective is to give all children a voice, not just the visual-spatial learner, but also any of the other frustrated and bewildered children who are currently learning math—including any parents who may be in this category. In addition to the they-don't-teach-it-the-way-I-learned-it quandary, parents could also feel the threat and frustration because they may not really understand the math having relied heavily on rote memorization to survive their own mathematics experiences. These loopholes leave parents to tread the math waters sans life jacket.

The visual-spatial learner benefits from knowing the larger context first, so that is the premise for this approach to organizing the information categories from a perspective of Big Idea sections named Definition, Organization, Relationships and Patterns, and Connections. Each section contains three chapters that clarify the Big Idea concerns faced by the visual, creative, mechanically minded, imaginative, curious child when given only verbal-sequential mathematics instruction. The final Conclusion chapter gives parents more hints and guidelines to help their children through this math homework challenge.

The math topics within these chapters are associated with grade levels as well as how the same topic appears and reappears in later mathematics or within other contexts. The grade levels are for guidelines only since curricula change in different schools, states, and regions. The idea is to explain the topic first visually and then show parents how the topic recycles throughout mathematics in different forms. Learning the math concept behind the topic appropriately *the first time* means that you do not have to relearn it.

The first chapter in the Definition section describes the origins of many of the terms that describe the "other" children who are *not* the verbal-sequential learners in a math class. The verbal-sequential learners are likely the achievers in a traditionally presented math program—a program that is generally formula-driven and consists of practiced and memorized information. The second chapter describes learning styles and intelligences with clues about how you can recognize these preferences and abilities in your child's math progress. The third chapter describes the problems behind reading mathematics information in different concepts.

The three chapters in the Organization section are focused on the ways that your child's mathematics understanding is assessed, presented, and arranged. The first chapter describes the intelligence tests that organize and monitor your child's progress and how they can miss the mark in measuring a visually dependent child's knowledge. The second chapter explores some of the problems with vision: the poor vision of physical sight, the inhibited vision of developmental processing, and the absence of vision in imagination. The third chapter provides an alternate method for thinking for your child to organize math problem information.

The Relationships and Patterns section describes three scenarios of math conditions: the scenario made up of those who hate or fear it, the Math Avoider; the scenario about those who like it, the Math Aficionado; and a third scenario describing those who are inspired by it through Insight. The chapters explain how a Math Avoider's psychological negativity is perpetuated, what the Math Aficionados know that Math Avoiders do not know (it isn't the math), and some stories about how children gained insight through different kinds of activities. Given the appropriate opportunities, your child can develop a new appreciation for *mathematical thinking*.

All students ask why they need to know math, some with wails and some with curiosity. The Connections section outlines three "artistic" areas where some of the "why" of mathematics can be answered: visual arts, choreography of dance and sports arts, and building artistry. The visual arts are explained through photography. The choreography or moving arts are developed with dance choreography and the physics in sports activities. The architecture and building arts contain some of the necessary mathematical arrangements that keep a structure upright.

Winning the Math Homework Challenge is not a how-to book with another process for calculating with math procedures. It is about visualizing math relationships. Ian Stewart describes three levels of math understanding. He tells us, "Formal mathematics is like spelling and grammar—a matter of the correct application of local rules. Meaningful mathematics is like journalism—it tells an interesting story.... The best mathematics is like literature—it brings a story to life before your eyes and involves you in it, intellectually and emotionally."[1] *Winning the Math Homework Challenge* starts the visual journey to bring patterns and connections to life.

The bibliography is not limited to the sources quoted or referenced in this book; the list embraces a broader range of sources that can be helpful for parents to investigate further in order to learn more about the ideas and activities in this book. Nor is it an exhaustive list, as that would possibly be as large and as extensive as an unabridged dictionary. Many of the early visionary math educators' references are included in this book because many of the current visual, imaginative, and creative activities can be traced back to their work.

Math unrest has been around for a long time, too long. Beginning over a century ago, Mary Everest Boole sought to make mathematics more understandable by utilizing instruction methods to involve children's imagination with hands-on materials. Fast-forward to 2012, when the Institute for Neuro-Innovation and Translational Neurosciences studied the neural correlates associated with math-anxiety. We are now well into the second decade of the twenty-first century, and the math anxiety malady is still with us. Is it really that unfixable? Maybe a part of the problem is that we aren't listening closely enough to our Math Avoider learners.

This book is not a math-made-easy book. Math isn't easy, but it *is* far simpler than its reputation as being complicated perceived by Math Avoiders. Math isn't flat after all, as one student observed; math has texture that you can grab onto. Thinking mathematically is the best mathematics and learning the best mathematics gives the satisfaction of winning a marathon of long-term connections and patterns, not running a sprint of shortcuts and sound bites.

"It was good enough for me" isn't working as a justification to keep the instruction the same. Same instruction while expecting different results has a dubious reputation. Linda Silverman and other researchers have found that the majority of the learning population has visual-spatial preferences for learning, a quantity that certainly requires some consideration for instructional changes. Drilling and memorization still exists, sometimes out of pure frustration, and neither is very helpful to learners, especially the visual learner. It is time to listen, listen beyond just the hearing.

NOTE

1. Hersch, *What Is Mathematics?*, iii.

Part I

DEFINITIONS

Spatial visualization and an interest in patterns are two of the most often noted interests of future mathematicians.[1] —Reuben Hersh and Vera John-Steiner

"They are waiting for me." This almost inaudible murmur was spoken by a single parent who was headed home after work to help with math homework. That unsettled feeling behind the murmur came from dreading if tonight would be the time when the math turned out to be "not the way I learned it." Another concerned parent expressed apprehension in another home, except that in the second house, the parent was clueless about why his child didn't understand because, to him, the math was so obvious. Both of these parents' attitudes had a significant impact on their children's learning.

As a homework-helping parent, you might be worried that word could get out that you cannot do your own child's math homework. Just one more confirmation that you can't do math, never could, and now you really resent it. Everyone will know your secret. In truth, you have more company than you realize. What if math never made sense to you because you are a visual learner? Maybe you memorized just to survive.

The first chapter in this section describes a variety of terms introduced over the decades to describe visualization, creative imagination, and other alternate thinking strategies. The second chapter focuses on how learning-style preference, natural thinking strategies, and special intelligences can make a significant difference in how your child experiences math. The last chapter explains how eye-tracking reading in math can be confusing because different eye-tracking directions are required for different math contexts. These three chapters in the Definitions section introduce some of the concerns surrounding learning mathematics.

Knowing about visual-spatial strengths is only part of the homework challenge. Being able to recognize when *your* child's visual strengths are not being addressed requires a different set of skills. Here are a few short vignettes about real children who have had difficulties in learning math. Each child had to conform the best way that they could. Lollie, Ned, Mary, and the other children in this section tell their stories. Your child might have had similar experiences.

Lollie, a personable first grader with a vivid imagination, had difficulty understanding the math lessons, her homework was torture, and she frequently daydreamed during class. At home, she designed and built machines that had specific purposes. For example, one of Lollie's machines could mix foods for dinner. The machine had several entry points for the ingredients, an exit spout for dinner, and a working turn handle. Her father followed her instructions as the "worker" to help her create the machine from cups, cardboard tubes, and a lot of tape.

Ned was already bored by second grade math practices with all the repeated practice problems. He liked to make up his own rules and solve math problems his own way—and he was usually accurate! Mary was a third grader who understood the math concept the first time and was extremely bored with the second explanation. While their personalities and ages were quite different, the result for both was boredom. Ned acted out while Mary simply found new things to do in math, making up new ideas as well as reading about new topics in mathematics books.

Lollie, Ned, Mary, and your child should have the opportunity to experience math relationships at their developmental level while utilizing their natural abilities. When you visualize math relationships, you can talk about it and refine it, but you cannot be marked "wrong." Visualization is a judgment-free zone. Maybe the missing pieces to understanding mathematics are explanations with visual-spatial descriptions.

NOTE

1. Hersh, *Loving + Hating Mathematics*, 21.

Chapter 1

A Rose Is Still a Rose—
Other Terms for Creativity

Creativity is intelligence having fun.[1] —Albert Einstein

You are the homework-helping parent coping with "new" procedures in what feels like "new" math. The math isn't new, but now there is a different way to "see" it. What if you *could* see the math relationships even if the procedures were different? Imagine for a moment what that would feel like. You may have been a visual learner who barely survived that secret math language, unable to use your visual abilities to learn math. Instead, your math experience was listening to *lots* of verbal instructions in a secret language. You and your child now have a chance to start seeing the math and talking about it in *your own way and in plain English*.

Your math experience may have been about survivalist tactics like memorizing formulas and fact tables. In actuality, those formulas and tables are the result of patterns and organizing shape areas, both visual and spatial characteristics. Philosophers and scientists have suggested the existence of "two brains" since the fourth century BC, when Diocles of Carystus wrote, "The [brain] lying on the right side is the one that perceives."[2] Fast-forward to the 1970s, when Roger Sperry introduced right hemisphere characteristics as part of his Nobel Prize–winning split-brain research. Others continue to study this "perceiving" brain function.

SOME OTHER WAYS TO "SEE" MATH

There are many ways to "see" mathematical relationships and just as many ways to express the "seeing" of those same mathematical relationships. Thinking mathematically does not always initially require calculations, but it *does* involve imagination, creativity, and, for many, visualization. The famed mathematician Henri Poincaré referred to "the unconscious work"[3] of mathematics thinking. He referred to utilizing symbols and logical thinking before and after, but not always during, visualization. If your child can use their spatial and "perceiving" abilities, then the math thinking and the communication will no longer feel like a secret language.

In the 1990s, Howard Gardner categorized and defined different intelligences. One was a visual-spatial intelligence, and another was a logical-mathematical intelligence. Gardner's visual-spatial learners use concept whole-to-part strategies to learn new material, such as visual images and classifications. They have a proclivity for doodling, sketching, and solving puzzles. His description for learners with the logical-mathematical intelligence includes ease with number and symbol calculations, a preference for sequential logic, and classifications. Both of these intelligences have functions associated with the right hemisphere regions of the brain.[4]

Over the decades, many authors have referred to this visual, imagination-oriented, and creative way of thinking as Thomas West did: "underappreciated in modern culture."[5] "A lamp to light your life"[6] was Alex Osborn's 1949 description for imagination, "lateral thinking" was coined by Edward de Bono in 1967, visual-mechanical strengths were described by John Dixon in 1983, and visual-spatial giftedness was researched by Linda Silverman in the 2000s. Roger von Oech encouraged "soft thinking"[7] as a strategy for creative thinking; David Lubinski referred to visualization as "a sleeping giant."[8]

All of these terms express ways of thinking that historically have not been a part of traditional step-by-step expository instruction methods for math. Edward de Bono's lateral thinking is all about looking for ways to see something "differently." John Dixon's visual-mechanical learners are adept with hands-on experimentation, are good with mental assembly, and have vibrant imaginations. Imagine being able to use *all* of these talents and abilities to learn what mathematics is really about. Your child's math creative imagination lamp is like a rose, and by any other name it is just as sweet.

VISUAL-SPATIAL AND AUDITORY-SEQUENTIAL

The simplest explanation of a visual-spatial learner is that they generally think in pictures, rather than in words. They also tend to learn holistically, instead of sequentially, or in parts. The visual-spatial learner can easily see the big picture of things, but might miss out on the details.[9]—Linda Silverman, PhD

The horizontal "number line graph" in Figure 1.1 shows the result of Silverman's research about two learning preferences, visual-spatial and verbal-sequential. Those with a visual-spatial preference make up approximately 63% of our school population, while the balance of less than 37% has a verbal-sequential preference. Of the visual-spatial learners, the 33.3% represented in the first bar show a strong visual-spatial preference. By comparison, the last bar shows that less than 25% are strongly verbal-sequential. Of those split in the middle who have a facility in both, about one-third still prefer visual and about 15% prefer auditory explanations.

If your child thinks in pictures like Temple Grandin or John Dixon, then the traditional written word or verbal-sequential presentation doesn't work. Grandin has often said, "I think in pictures. Words are like a second language to me."[10] Also, Dixon's young thoughts about his classmates describe the experience of too many children: "As I looked around at my classmates, their ease at turning written words into the

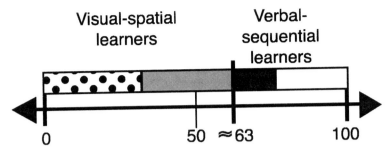

Figure 1.1

correct spoken words seemed to [mean that] ... they possessed a secret wisdom to which I was not privy."[11]

While Grandin specifically addresses the autism and Asperser's syndrome, the preference for visual-spatial thinking constitutes a majority of the *total* population, including the gifted learners in Dixon's population and the gifted dyslexic creative thinkers profiled by West. Imagine how it might feel to be a visual-spatial learner and have to translate everything from spatial images to words *before* writing or saying anything in math. Under these circumstances, you might be dubbed "slow at math" and evolve into a Math Avoider. "Mount Visual Translation" is a very high mountain to climb.

Imagine the work that this translation would require; imagine the *time it would take*. No wonder these visual-spatial learners have trouble keeping up with the verbal-sequential learners! Just imagine how they would react to a timed test page filled with "basic math" facts! As a parent, you may be one of these visual-spatial learners grown up; your child may be one of these visual-spatial school children currently in a math class. The extra time required for translation combined with the "slow at math life sentence" will surely trigger Math Avoidance behavior *and* a math anxiety. Another mountain to get over or around: "Mount Slow-At-Math."

While the early K–2 grades tend to include more hands-on activities as part of the math instruction for children to learn about math relationships, things change around the third grade, when, unfortunately, play ends and schools get serious about the formal math curriculum, critically serious for the visual-spatial learner. Clearly, we need more "spatial culture at all age [levels],"[12] as Alsina encourages, not just in the early grades.

When visual-spatial learners are only exposed to step-by-step math instruction, they daydream and enjoy their own imaginations, two strategies intrinsically valuable to mathematics but lethal for following directions. These learners, like Lollie, could become mentally isolated and secluded, possibly ending up at the back of the room where they peacefully daydream but miss out on math instruction. On the other hand, if auditory-sequential learners don't learn the Big Ideas to jump-start their imaginations, then they miss out on the creative lamp-lighting kind of math problem-solving. Mathematics loses when either of these situations happens.

Lesley Sword is another author who has worked extensively with visual-spatial learners. Her article, "I Think in Pictures, You Teach in Words: The Gifted Visual-Spatial Learner," describes several visual-spatial learners who face the dilemma of receiving only sequential step-by-step verbal instruction in math. There is a solution to this dilemma. Provide your child with both kinds of instruction to engage their imagination, provide creative outlets, and give them an overall context *along with* any familiar expository step-by-step instruction. Both types of learners will benefit *and* mathematics wins.

John Dixon assigned the term "spatial children" to those children who have specialized spatial and mechanical strengths.[13] In his book, *The Spatial Child*, Dixon tells the stories about school-challenged people who succeeded when their instruction was changed, specifically two children, Reuben and Nilda, who were originally diagnosed as special needs but who thrived with spatial learning methods. Thomas West profiled several nonconforming, visually motivated, Nobel Prize–winning scientists who changed the world. Both Dixon and West use spatial and spatial-mechanical descriptions when referring to visual ways of thinking and perceiving.

There is a very real need to include visual-spatial learning techniques with any verbal-sequential expository math instruction so that more children, including your child, can understand more mathematics. For the visual-spatial learner, a visual explanation may be the missing link. Imagine how a visual learner might feel to finally have that "aha moment" of understanding, of "getting it," because they can *see* the math relationships and purpose instead of struggle with what they see as random, separated, and disjointed pieces of math.

Your child should have the opportunity to use *all* of their abilities to work on any problem-solving task, the creative aspect of envisioning math concepts along with lateral thinking strategies mixed with an expertise for analyzing, organizing, and writing. Whichever naturally comes first, imagination *and* communication are necessary to avoid a lopsided view of math. The noted mathematician Benoit Mandelbrot is said to have looked at equations and envisioned pictures, and Albert Einstein reportedly imagined pictures and wrote equations. It takes a mix of different ways of thinking in order to *really* see and communicate mathematics.

KEEP IN MIND

Mathematics is not restricted to just one kind of thinking or one side of the brain thinking. We have one brain with a variety of different specialties. As Robert Ornstein points out, "It's [about] an understanding of meaning, the small meaning of events and the overall meaning of the situation. We can't have the big meaning of things without the small."[14] Sperry's left-hemisphere thinking *is* capable of creativity and insightful leaps just as the right hemisphere is; your child should be encouraged to use *both*, the overall understanding and the details, to their advantage.

Visual-spatial thinking requires "an active exploration, selection, grasping of essentials, simplification, abstraction, analysis, and synthesis, completion, correction, comparison, and problem solving. As well as combining, separating, and putting in context."[15] This just about covers any concerns that might arise about a connection between visual thinking and critical thinking in mathematics.

Your child can put all of their imaginative abilities to work by using household items repurposed for some mathematics learning. The "Think of a Number" puzzle in Figure 1.2 shows how disks and square tiles can help your child "see" three versions for communicating math: words, pictures, and symbols. The square tile represents the number that you are thinking of but not telling anyone. The round chip represents the number of items specified in the instruction to be added, subtracted, multiplied, or divided. Awaken your child's sleeping giant imagination and creativity within!

Think of a Number Puzzle

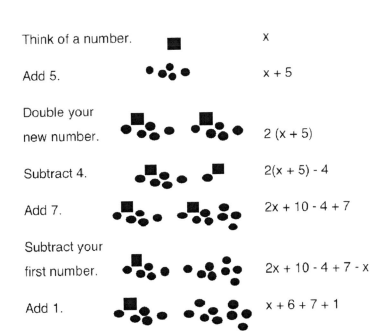

Think of a number.	■	x
Add 5.	••••	x + 5
Double your new number.	■••• ■•••	2 (x + 5)
Subtract 4.	■••• ■•	2(x + 5) - 4
Add 7.	■••• ■••••	2x + 10 - 4 + 7
Subtract your first number.	■••• ••••	2x + 10 - 4 + 7 - x
Add 1.	■••• ••••	x + 6 + 7 + 1
Subtract your first number again.	•••• ••••	x + 6 + 7 - x + 1
Your answer is 14.		14

How do you suppose this happens?

Figure 1.2

NOTES

1. http://www.goodreads.com/quotes/37706-creativity-is-intelligence-having-fun.
2. Ornstein, *The Right Mind*, 44.
3. Osborn, *Your Creative Power*, 237.
4. Armstrong, *Multiple Intelligences in the Classroom*, 7.
5. West, *Thinking Like Einstein*, 40.
6. Osborn, *Your Creative Power*, 1.

7. von Oech, *Whack on the Side of the Head*, 29.

8. Lubinski, *Spatial Ability and STEM*, 344.

9. Silverman, *Upside Down Brilliance*, https://www.time4learning.com/visual-spatial-learners.shtml.

10. Grandin, *Thinking in Pictures*, 1.

11. Dixon, *The Spatial Child*, 8.

12. Alsina, *Math Made Visual*, 125.

13. Dixon, *The Spatial Child*, 5.

14. Ornstein, *The Right Mind*, 158.

15. Alsina, *Math Made Visual*, 122.

Chapter 2

Learning Styles, Learning Networks, and Learning Intelligences

The average human brain has 100 billion neurons, each with about 10,000 connections with other neurons for thinking thoughts. This total number of connections could easily outnumber the total of fiber optic "connections" in your Internet delivery service. That means your child's brain is more powerful than fiber optic delivery networks!

Our neurons make it possible to see, feel, hear, smell, and taste at the same time while they manage heartbeat and breathing. What they cannot do is make your child see, feel, hear, smell, or taste and understand the same way that you do. The chance of getting an exact match between your child's 100 billion neurons to your 100 billion neurons is quite slim. You *can* nurture, encourage, and lead your child toward understanding math through their own neurological connections. Capitalizing on your child's innate abilities and preferred learning styles will make learning mathematics make more sense for both of you.

Parents ask, "How can I encourage my child's talents, specifically in math?" If your child has some specific abilities, then it would clearly make sense to use them in their learning experiences, which also incorporates their preferred learning styles. Learning styles are preferences for learning and intelligences are proclivities for special abilities. Your child has both, maybe even several of both. With all of those powerful neurons making connections inside your child's brain, wouldn't it make sense to use the most effective and efficient means, both learning style and intelligences, to prop up their mathematics learning?

LEARNING STYLES

Learning style identification has been around for several decades. Your child and other children learn at different paces and through different kinds of activities. Rita and Kenneth Dunn developed a comprehensive assessment instrument called the Learning Style Inventory[1] that identified four major stimuli that affected a child's achievement; each stimulus consisted of four to six components covering environmental, emotional, sociological, and physical elements. Their individual profile instrument is used to provide a very detailed outline for a child's optimum learning environment.

In her 1992 book *Learning Styles*, Priscilla Vail introduced a different frame of reference for interpreting learning styles. Vail categorized styles for learning into four sections: availability for schoolwork, learning through three-dimensional or two-dimensional materials, simultaneous or sequential thinker, and multisensory experiences. Each of these styles was further described through four additional learning conditions: does the child initiate action, can the child sustain attention, is the child easily distracted, and can the child shift focus from one topic to another.[2]

An example of a neurologically based diagnostic math instrument that addresses students' math strengths as well as learning preferences is the *Mathematics Diagnostic Prescriptive Inventory* (MDPI).[3] Maria Marolda, Ellen Boiselle, and Patricia Davidson developed the MDPI to evaluate a child's mathematics strengths *and* how they reason. The different models used during the assessment process allow a child to use their unique abilities and specific reasoning processes. The MDPI results provide a profile of the child within two descriptive learning preferences: whole gestalt or sequential detail.

Educators and psychologists are still contributing to the concept of identifying ideal and preferred learning environments, a movement that in the long term produces positive *and* productive results for learners. In addition to the Dunn's instrument, Vail's components, and Marolda, Boiselle, and Davidson's MDPI, Anthony Gregorc developed a Mind Styles model[4] in the 1980s that is still available. The model describes modes of thinking in a four-sector arrangement using a two-pole axis organizer with Concrete Thinker and Abstract Thinker on the vertical axes crossed with Sequential Organizer and Random Organizer on the horizontal axis.

LEARNING NETWORKS

Learning Network theory and other brain-based learning theories have a benefit of twenty-first-century neurological knowledge and technology that can enhance earlier works. During the 1950s "post Sputnik Period," Benjamin Bloom developed Bloom's Taxonomy and Robert Gagne created an Instructional Design hierarchy. Jean Piaget and Bärbel Inhelder researched children's learning development that culminated in their Four Stages of Child Development: Sensorimotor, Preoperational, Concrete Operational, and Formal Operational. Others continue to contribute to this ongoing, constantly evolving process of education and human development.

Advancing technology has provided unprecedented access to large amounts of synthesized information previously unavailable in the search for the best approaches to educate our children. This information has furnished researchers, educators, neurologists, and psychologists with the breadth of statistics that can guide and advance their progress toward identifying and improving the best efforts to educate children and nurture human development.

LEARNING INTELLIGENCES

Howard Gardner introduced the concept of seven intelligences and later included an eighth: Body-Kinesthetic—the dancers, sports players, and builders/carpenters;

Interpersonal—the talkers, possibly leaders, and actors; Intrapersonal—the thinkers, feelers, and imaginative daydreamers; Musical—the musicians, song writers, and composers; Spatial—the artists, designers, and metaphor describers; Linguists—the writers, orators, and debaters; Mathematics—the number pattern identifiers, geometry classifiers, and data analyzers; and Naturalists—the nature walkers, biologists, and rock collectors. How can these intelligences affect math topics?

Body-Kinesthetic

Instead of trying to verbally explain the elements of a circle, circumference, diameter, radius, arc, and degrees of angles, work with your child to build a large model demonstrating these elements. Use a very long piece of material such as yarn, long strips of sail canvas cutoffs from a boatyard, or torn strips from a tattered sheet. This model could also serve as a musical-chairs-type path for identifying locations on the circumference, such as clock time locations or angle locations. As long as the music plays, your child walks on the path. The location labels on the circle will depend on the grade level or your imagination (or your child's imagination).

High-school students can walk to a musical chair tune to name radian locations on a circle, middle-school students can identify angle locations referenced from the 0° mark, and younger students can identify time locations on a clock. You can make this "music walking game" more interesting or challenging by using combinations of circle shapes such as a snowman, a clock without hours, or a circle with only a few angle references, as shown in Figure 2.1. When the music stops, your child can answer questions like "What time is it where you stand?" or "What is the angle measure where you stand?"

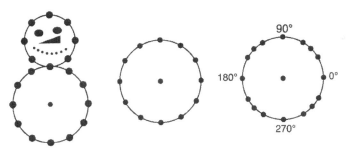

Figure 2.1   Some musical walking paths.

Interpersonal

Instead of trying to explain the details about the differences in types of numbers, let your interpersonal-intelligence child role-play (or describe) a fantasy story about how a whole-number inhabitant might feel when thrust into a world called *Imaginary Numberland* or *Fractionland*. A younger child can write a play about an integer (or whole number or ratio number) astronaut who launches from an integer planet (or whole-number planet or ratio planet) and lands on another planet where only decimals live. They can include all of the mystery, searching for food, and any other survival tactics that the "aliens" might require to survive on the planet.

A second grader named Deirdre wrote a play using details from her imaginary dream instead of an astronaut landing on another planet. Her names for the inhabitants in her dream included "Plusses" and "Minuses" led by Mr. Pattern as the protagonist and Nonsense as the antagonist. Deirdre's mystery play included rich details of each character and clever solutions for how to resolve the math problem mysteries in her dream. Deirdre's play ended when her mom called to wake her. Your playwright child can write a drama, a comedy, or a mystery.

Intrapersonal

Instead of trying to explain division for a math problem, let your child generate at least three creative methods for completing a division problem. You provide the "answer" along with the original numbers in the division problem. Let your child write different ways in which the problem could be "computed." Asking for three methods keeps your child from thinking that you want "the right method" instead of their creation. Your child's imagination will really kick in when trying to come up with those two extra methods. You can provide the division problem and the result, or you could provide all three numbers and let your child decide which one is the "answer."

Musical

Instead of showing your musically talented child how to find a lowest common denominator for fractions, let them listen to tempos for whole notes, half notes, quarter notes, and eighth notes and write a rap song that uses these tempos. They can figure out how the notes are counted and what the difference is between a quarter note and a three-quarter note. Are all of these notes common to the quarter note? Why do these beats work together? Bill used three intelligences to write a rap (tempo) poem (linguistic) to share how a square (spatial) might feel.

It Ain't Easy Being A Square

It ain't easy being a square.
With all those restrictions, it's just not fair.
To be so congruent just seems so rare.
It ain't easy being a square.

The hierarchy is large with me on top.
I wish I was home plate or the sign that reads "Stop."
The other shapes are so unique—I feel like a flop
When the hierarchy is large with me on top.

My angles are 90 degrees and my sides are the same.
To always complain just seems so vain.
But to figure one out, you don't need a brain
Cause my angles are 90 degrees and my sides are the same.

No, it's not easy being a square.
I want different angles, at least one pair.
To stay so congruent, I just couldn't bare [*sic*].
Man, it ain't easy being a square.

Spatial

Instead of talking about fractions, let your "designer" child make a collage of a fraction like Jamie's three-fourths poster shown in Figure 2.2. Jamie loved to draw, could design any outfit for any occasion, and was a daydreamer extraordinaire. The chapter was about fractions with all of the typical pictures, with the counting of wholes and comparing them with the parts. Jamie's fraction interpretation for three-fourths was to find lots of examples that had four in the original set and remove or change one in the set. Three Beatles, three light switches turned off, and three pieces of pizza in the pan are just a few that she used.

Figure 2.2 Jamie's poster.

Linguists

Instead of explaining about the properties of shapes, ask your child to write a poem incorporating shapes like Kim's poem about the "ultimate purpose" of a rectangle. Kim used a mix of empathy feelings and shape properties to spell "Rectangle" on opposite parallel sides of her poem shown in Figure 2.3. Song lyrics, poetry, and plays are only three of the ways in which linguist-intelligent writers can describe shapes, numbers, and other mathematical concepts. Two linguist-intelligent mathematicians— Edwin Abbot, author of *Flatland*, and Charles Dodgson (AKA Lewis Carroll), author of *Alice's Adventures in Wonderland*—shared their math ideas through stories.

The Rectangle

*R*eaching   further   than   the   average   squar*E*

*E*qual   opposites   –   four   that   are   paralle*L*

*C*onservative, controlled   –   honored shape of our fla*G*

*T*eeming high above rooftops waving in the su*N*

*A*lways an eye to see the beauty of Americ*A*

*N*eeding only a pane so clear made tight to fi*T*

*G*iving pride to our hearts – making our life ti*C*

*L*arge or small – seeing it narrow or wid*E*

*E*very rectangle is proud, knows what its purpose is fo*R*

Figure 2.3

Mathematical

If your math explanations are making sense to your math-intelligent child, then don't change them because you are already talking to a Math Aficionado. However, enhance some of your explanations with a few drawings. For example, recognizing patterns is an essential part of good mathematical thinking, so try drawing some patterns with a number association. The letter "E" example in Figure 2.4 shows how two ends of the "E" grow at a regular rate and generate a pattern. Start with any letter, use a specific number to change the design, and generate a new version of the letter. Take turns. Let your child create with their imagination.

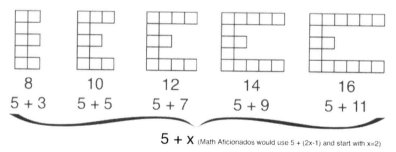

| 8 | 10 | 12 | 14 | 16 |
| 5 + 3 | 5 + 5 | 5 + 7 | 5 + 9 | 5 + 11 |

$5 + X$ (Math Aficionados would use 5 + (2x-1) and start with x=2)

Figure 2.4

Naturalists

Instead of explaining about symmetry, go on a nature walk with your naturalist child and look for examples of symmetry in leaves (both sides match). Look for other patterns like concentric circles (all circles have the same center) in cross sections of tree trunks, repeating patterns in a spider web, and rotational symmetry in flower petals like the ones in Figure 2.5. Take photos of these items. Search for symmetry in shells while walking on the beach in a nice weather. For indoor weather naturalist projects, your child can look for pictures of these natural items and make a symmetry collage or a pictograph of the different categories.

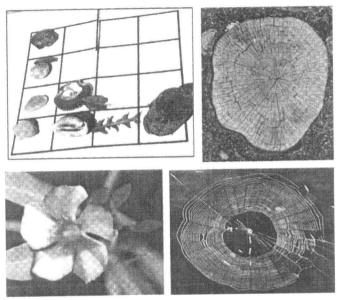

Figure 2.5 *Source*: Spider photo by Marcia Perry.

LEARNING PREFERENCES THROUGH THE SENSES

Now let's go back in time to Confucius in the fifth and sixth century BC for what could have been the very first description of learning styles. He is credited with the famous proverb, "I hear and I forget, I see and I remember, and I do then I understand," but the proverb really belongs to Xunzi, a fellow reformer. Regardless of who may have said it, the truth of it is in the practice. These three senses, hearing, seeing and touching, represent three of the five senses and show the sensory input range from passive hearing to a more active involvement.

If your child learns best through hearing, then they may be in good shape by just listening to an explanation. If your child must see the relationships, then they need more and different visual explanations beyond the telling. If your child is a hands-on learner, then they cannot understand without involvement. These sensory inputs may or may not be interdependent. The sight learner may or may not need the verbal instructions. The hands-on learner may or may not need a diagram, like the hands-on child that grew up to be a hands-on parent who assembles the bicycle without reading the instructions.

For mathematics, the "seeing sense" too often takes a back seat to the "hearing sense." If symbolic scribbles on a chalkboard are the only ways provided for the "seeing sense," then the visual-spatial learner is doubly "passived-out" of the learning process. If the abstract verbal-sequential linear thinker Math Aficionado helps the non-linear visual-spatial mechanical learner with only left-brain auditory instruction, then the results are probably the ones we read about in the math phobia self-help books. A mouthful of problems and mountain-climbing-like difficulties for the spatial-creative-imaginative hands-on child!

There is more to visual-spatial learning than just including pictures and diagrams in explanations, although pictures and diagrams have a significant impact. The visual-spatial learner needs the whole idea, the relationship, and the general drift of the topic before they are interested in the details, the explanations, or the sequential logical arguments supporting the concept. Making comparisons, using imagination, capitalizing on intuition, and exploring the big picture of Big Idea concepts are good ways to engage your visual-spatial child.

Since comparisons, intuition, imagination, and Big Idea strategies are also valuable to the auditory-sequential learners, your child will benefit whether or not they are strongly visual, strongly auditory, or have both strengths. Ever since Roger Sperry's split-brain work, math educators have worked to involve the strengths from both hemispheres in mathematics learning experiences. Having both hemispheres involved means that concepts cross over the 300 million nerve fibers in the corpus callosum "Great-Divide" connecting the left-hemisphere linear sequential logic to the right-hemisphere sensitive, analogical, whole-to-part context preferences.

Confucius and Xunzi provided the proverb and math educators and parents can provide the material for implementing the proverb as it applies to math. Mathematics tends to be treated as an abstract manipulation of symbols recognized and understood only by the chosen few Math Aficionados. Mathematics, too often, is presented in such a manner that "only those with a secret wisdom" can earn the "eyes of pleasure"[5] from teachers and parents. The good news is that this wisdom is no longer secret because now your child can use three of their five senses to learn mathematics: hearing, seeing, and touching.

SEEING RELATIONSHIPS WITH YOUR HANDS

Being able to move data around as represented by shapes helps the visual-spatial learner "get their hands on" the relationships between and among the data. Anytime that your visual child can literally move the data, information, or shapes, the better chance they have of making their own sense of the math instructions. This moving around gives them control and a chance to see how another arrangement might work—or not work. Having "permission" to remove information from a fixed spot on a sheet of paper and rearrange it makes a significant difference in how your child can recognize mathematical relationships.

One example for moving data can be experienced with graphed data in preparation for statistical calculations. Graphs communicate number relationships visually. Your child began to learn about graphs early in their elementary journey, most likely by keeping records of rainy, sunny, and cloudy days. By fourth or fifth grade, your child started averaging data for the numbers in the graphs. Data arrangement and geometry can be connected because the average (mean) of the data can be represented with congruent pieces.

Visualize a bar graph of data like the one in Figure 2.6. If your child is younger, then they might enjoy using keys to make a "pre-bar graph" or pictograph. By using cubes or any shape to make a graph bar, your child will experience how objects in three dimensions can convert to a two-dimensional graph on a piece of paper. The keys in the key pictograph in Figure 2.6 will eventually need to be associated with the cubes (or a square on a grid), one key to one cube, so that the graph bars can have a standard measure.

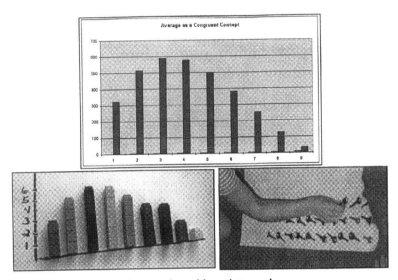

Figure 2.6   Bar graph, linking cubes graph, and key pictograph.

To calculate the average, or mean, of data amounts, first add all of the amounts in the bars and then divide by the number of bars in the original graph. The visual hands-on version of this relationship is to first remove the bars or cubes from the graph (or trace the bars separately) and connect all of the cube lengths into one long "lightsaber" (or tape the traced paper bars end to end). This assembly is the addition part. Next, separate the "lightsaber" stick of cubes into equal lengths (or fold the long paper strip), as shown in Figure 2.7. The separation (or fold) is the division part. The separated cubes (or cut pieces of paper) of the individual pieces have equal lengths.

Folding the strip into nine equal pieces, or breaking into nine equal sections, is the visual hands-on version of dividing by nine. After cutting the folded pieces, your child would replace each of these bars with the new length on the old graph layout—the average length for all nine bars is represented by the nine equal pieces. One of those equally broken bars or folded papers represents the average-sized piece, or the calculated average or the mean of the data. It is also the "answer" to a division problem. The graph of the averages in Figure 2.8 shows how the "average" cube lengths and the folded paper lengths are rearranged as averages on a graph.

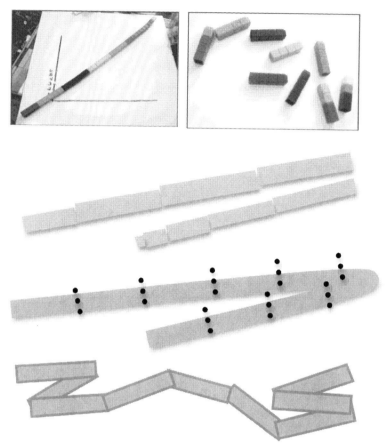

Figure 2.7

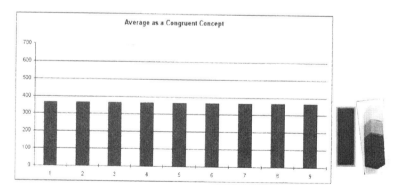

Figure 2.8

Another way to see the redistribution of the graph bars to show a hands-on average representation is to cut off and literally rearrange the lengths until all bars are the same length. Represent this redistribution of the lengths of the bars by removing pieces from the tops of the taller bars to build up the smaller bars until all are bars are the same length as shown in Figure 2.9. Your child would continue cutting and pasting (or rearranging the linking cubes) until all of the bars are the same length.

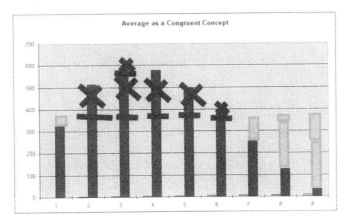

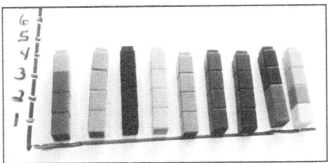

Figure 2.9   Average after rearranging.

SEEING PATTERNS WITH YOUR IMAGINATION

An example of taking an ordinarily boring fact learning task involves making patterns with either the 100s chart or a multiplication table. The pattern idea can also be applied to an addition table. The grids in Figure 2.10 show number patterns that go with a 100s chart. The different pattern grids represent the patterns for the twos, the threes, the fours, the fives, the sixes, and the nines. Provide a blank ten-by-ten grid sheet so that your child can color the grids themselves to make their own patterns. Or, if you both prefer, use a ten-by-ten 100s chart with the numbers so that your child can see the numbers while they color the patterns.

100 Chart

1	2	3	4	5	6	7	8	9	10
11	12	13	14	15	16	17	18	19	20
21	22	23	24	25	26	27	28	29	30
31	32	33	34	35	36	37	38	39	40
41	42	43	44	45	46	47	48	49	50
51	52	53	54	55	56	57	58	59	60
61	62	63	64	65	66	67	68	69	70
71	72	73	74	75	76	77	78	79	80
81	82	83	84	85	86	87	88	89	90
91	92	93	94	95	96	97	98	99	100

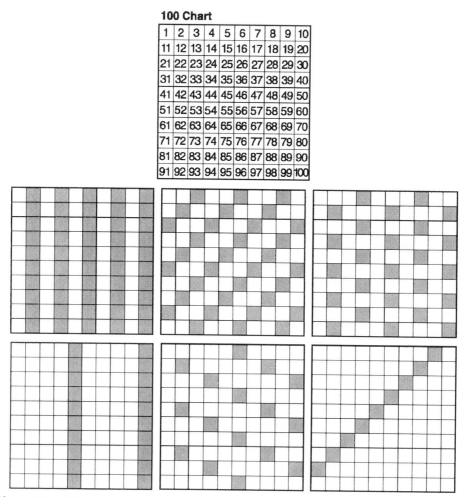

Figure 2.10   100s chart patterns.

The pattern grids in Figure 2.11 show the designs that match the multiplication table. These patterns show the multiples of twos, threes, fours, fives, sixes, and nines. By comparing the patterns, your child can identify connections between the designs that match the number patterns. Your visual-spatial creative child might enjoy coloring the rest of the multiple designs for the sevens, eights, and tens and then comparing these designs with others or using an addition table to color different designs.

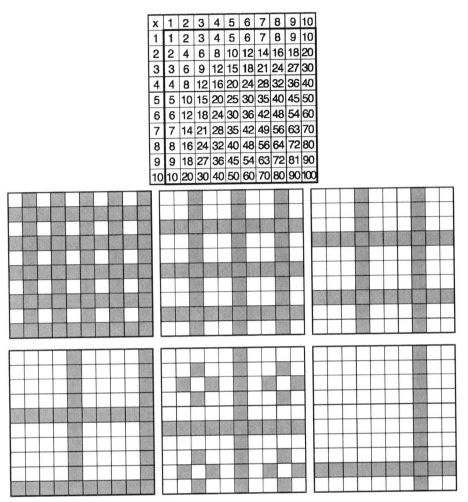

x	1	2	3	4	5	6	7	8	9	10
1	1	2	3	4	5	6	7	8	9	10
2	2	4	6	8	10	12	14	16	18	20
3	3	6	9	12	15	18	21	24	27	30
4	4	8	12	16	20	24	28	32	36	40
5	5	10	15	20	25	30	35	40	45	50
6	6	12	18	24	30	36	42	48	54	60
7	7	14	21	28	35	42	49	56	63	70
8	8	16	24	32	40	48	56	64	72	80
9	9	18	27	36	45	54	63	72	81	90
10	10	20	30	40	50	60	70	80	90	100

Figure 2.11   Multiplication table patterns.

The designs from the 100s chart and the multiplication table are distinctively different from each other. One chart has some diagonal patterns and the other has more vertical and horizontal patterns. You can make a game out of guessing the patterns from a deck of pattern cards that your child makes. Make it really challenging by mixing the pattern cards from both charts and tables. Some visual learners prefer to guess the patterns without the numbers. You and your child get to choose. Do not say or do anything that your child can say or do. If you do, you are interrupting their thinking, their own kind of learning, and valuable problem-solving.

To provide one of those imagination opportunities, your child can make up some of their own patterns on a blank ten-by-ten square grid sheet. Maybe your child's grid patterns will match up to numbers on a 100s chart or a multiplication table. A third grader named Li created an example of a unique pattern shown in Figure 2.12. Her design was from her imagination and the 100s chart. Li described her pattern using numbers with, "two, two, six, six, two, two." Li could also have used just the tens digits for a pattern: 20, 20, 30, 30, 40, 40, 40, 40, 40, 40, 50, 50, 50, 50, 50, 50, 60, 60, 70, 70 or another version of the sequence from the 100s chart.

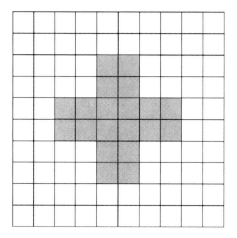

Figure 2.12   Li's design.

KEEP IN MIND

Think of a child's developmental learning levels as being like a butterfly's growth stages. Both have four stages to go through for full and beautiful expression. If they aren't ready, then they can't—a cocoon cannot fly any more than a child at the pre-operational level can deal with abstract symbolism. Learning styles, abilities, and talents nurture your child's mathematics learning. With the appropriate opportunities and experiences provided when they are ready, your child will be able to fly like a butterfly with their math.

One size does *not* fit all. Learning is personal. Use your best parent "pleasing eyes" to encourage your child to use as many of their learning preferences, neural nets, and intelligences as possible. Your child has several intelligence abilities and maybe more than a few learning-style combinations for their optimum learning environment. A Quick Flip Activities tool[6] for hemisphere and critical thinking ideas is available in many retail and Internet locations that can help you help your child find their Math Mojo through their own special talents. Your child needs to know that there *is* a possible way to translate math into their way of thinking.

NOTES

1. Dunn, *Teaching Students Through Their Individual Learning Styles*, 4.

2. Vail, *Learning Styles*, 3–5.

3. Marolda, *Mathematics Diagnostic Prescriptive Inventory*, http://www.mathdiagnostics. com/math_diagnostics_web_30_may_12_005.htm.

4. Gregorc, http://www.ccconline.org/gregorcs-mind-styles-model/.

5. Dixon, *The Spatial Child*, 5.

6. http://www.amazon.com/Quick-Flip-Activities-Multiple-Intelligences/dp/1564724905.

Chapter 3

GPS for Reading Math

Second star to the right and straight on 'til morning. —J. M. Barrie, *Peter Pan*

"My child gets confused easily, what should I do?" Check if your child is eye-tracking the math (reading in the appropriate direction) before you try to explain anything. You and your child may not be looking at the same thing. For example, your child spends a great deal of time and effort to learn how to decipher written words and then to interpret a long string of written word symbols as having a message, always going from left-to-right. Along comes math place value, when your child learns how to build numbers working from right-to-left as the single-digit placements increase the number value. No wonder your child can get confused.

In fact, the reading eye-tracking directions change quite frequently in reading math symbols and models. Eye-tracking changes in mathematics can make all of us learning-challenged if we do not know which way to track our eyes. This excerpt might describe how your child could be thinking: "My reading teacher has been telling me to track left to right and I have been doing this in all of those books in the reading corner. In math class, I am supposed to add beginning on the right and then go left, but I have to convince them that I *can* still get an accurate result if I start on the left and go right as long as I keep up with the regrouping."

Their reasoning continues: "Now I have to read that round thing called a clock. I can still go left-to-right around but then I end up back where I started. They are not even using the numbers that I see on the round clock when they say minutes but I'll figure that out later. For now I have to figure out how I am going to read the time from left-to-right and then after I pass the number on the bottom, say the correct time using both directions like 'seven forty-five' or 'fifteen minutes to eight.'" Your child might think this and remain silent, so it is up to you to intercept this line of reasoning before it gets out of hand and totally disheartening.

There are at least eight different directional eye-track reading directions in math, and that is before dizzying combinations of these directions are brought into the mix for computation procedures and calculations. The eye-tracking change combinations can feel like a visual quagmire to your child if the directions change without warning. The eye-tracking GPS directions in this chapter cover: straight line reading left-to-right, straight line reading right-to-left, around left-to-right and then reversed in the other direction, top-to-bottom, bottom-to-top, diagonal left-to-right, and diagonal right-to-left. Then straight on 'til morning.

STRAIGHT LINE LEFT-TO-RIGHT AND RIGHT-TO-LEFT

The eye-tracking direction for reading a number is left-to-right, the same direction for reading word sentences. Numbers are read by saying the headings in place value *with* each number digit as shown with the "357" number in Figure 3.1, which is read "three hundred fifty-seven," also left-to-right. However, when your child is *building* the number in categories from one to ten, and then to hundred, they must start on the right and build in a right-to-left direction. Not only is your child learning *when* to swap the blocks to different categories, but they are also learning *how* to build and reassemble the numbers in the reverse direction.

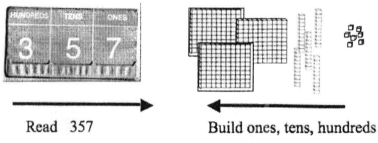

Read   357   Build ones, tens, hundreds

Figure 3.1

AROUND LEFT-TO-RIGHT AND THEN REVERSED

Analog clocks, circle graphs, fraction diagrams, and reading angle degrees are only four of many topics that can pose yet another eye-tracking change and challenge. The directional reading is both right-to-left and left-to-right in a rounded direction as shown in Figure 3.2 with the dotted lines. Sometimes the two directions must happen at the same time as the hands move on the clock, such as reading three o'clock, three forty-five, or backward as in fifteen minutes before three. To read and interpret these four circular contexts, your child is faced with the same mix of eye-tracking in both directions, all happening simultaneously.

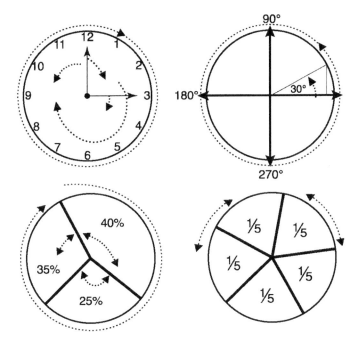

Figure 3.2

TOP-TO-BOTTOM AND BOTTOM-TO-TOP

Soon after your child gets used to the left-right and right-left eye-tracking directions for reading numbers and the circular directions for clocks, the eye-tracking reading math direction changes again for reading and interpreting fraction notations. Fractions are read top-down as shown with the dotted lines in Figure 3.3 and should be read in such a way that will include the division bar as often as possible, such as "3 divided by 4." A creative third grader named Joy described the two dots in the division symbol as "the two unborn numbers in a fraction." If it is a fraction, then something has been broken apart, shared, or separated or, in other words, divided.

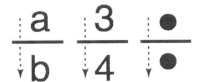

Figure 3.3

DIAGONAL LEFT-TO-RIGHT AND DIAGONAL RIGHT-TO-LEFT

Some of the examples of reading diagonally in mathematics are illustrated in Figure 3.4 showing how to read those math tables for addition and multiplication. Children are not always developmentally ready for reading in more than one direction at a time when the addition table appears or the multiplication table appears on the math scene. And if the tables weren't enough, mixed numbers, numbers with exponents, division problems, and the cross multiplication strategy used with proportions to keep fractions balanced, all require a diagonal direction. Eye-tracking directional reading liabilities do not end in first, second, or even third grade!

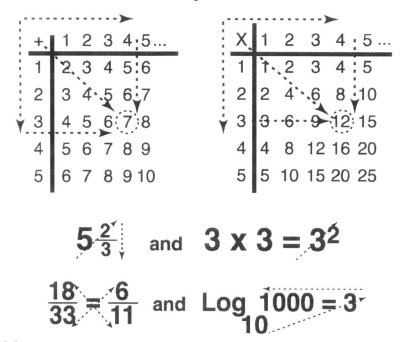

Figure 3.4

EYE-TRACKING COMBINATIONS

Even if the diagonal reading directions did not cause confusion, a long-division example or a two-digit multiplication problem like the ones in Figure 3.5 surely will. If an Eye-Tracking Patrol existed, long division would be arrested by now. Division and multiplication algorithm examples aren't the only problematic reading examples that present reading difficulties, but they are quite challenging for many. Track your own eyes and processing for reading a long-division problem, but this time make the problem have a remainder. Then call the Eye-Tracking Patrol!

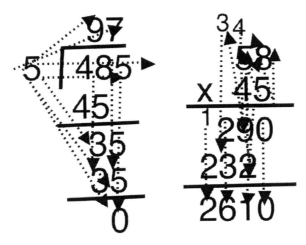

Figure 3.5

Interpreting graphs like the ones in Figure 3.6 can also present eye-tracking head-aches because multiple eye-tracking directions are required. In elementary grades, your child learned to read pictographs, bar graphs, and line graphs all requiring a left-to-right direction combined with a bottom-to-top direction. The coordinate axes grid shown in Figure 3.6 presents a particular eye-tracking problem because the up-down direction is combined with straight line left-to-right direction while keeping another sequence of order for the x and y for coordinate point locations. This can feel like an eyesight roller coaster!

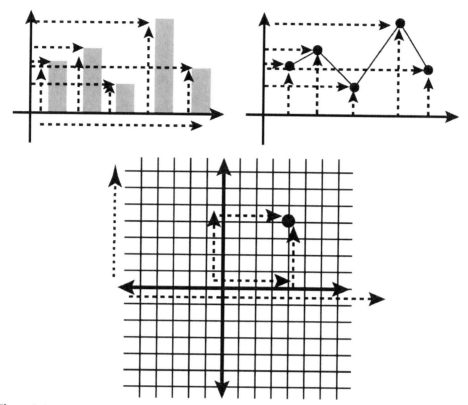

Figure 3.6

KEEP IN MIND

If your child cannot see what you or the teacher is talking about or is following a different eye-tracking direction, then confusion around the math concept or topic will likely be the result. Many times using a highlighter can help your child with the eye-tracking directions by using different colors for different directions. Mathematics may not be Neverland, but the directions can be easier to follow if your child knows where and how to look.

Part II

ORGANIZATION

Sometimes the most brilliant and intelligent minds do not shine in standardized tests because they don't have standardized minds.[1] —Diane Ravitch

Syd memorized the facts in third grade in order to pass that three-minute rite-of-passage test and then promptly forgot them. She preferred to use her fingers; in fact, she was pretty fast with her fingers. The argument that memorization of the "facts" provided a faster way to solve math problems fell deaf on her ears because Syd's fingers were far more reliable than those memorized facts. She had survived most of her elementary math topics; yet now she was flunking eighth grade math. Despite her poor math scores, Syd's thinking around math topics was clearly all about the Big Ideas in math and not about the small calculation details.

Tests are organized around what they are supposed to measure, whether for intelligence quotients, achievement, progress, or abilities. Each test has a specific function and the data collected from these tests provides a statistical snapshot of how your child fits into the learning structure. Collecting data is the scientific way to analyze results. How you use this collected data to your child's advantage toward improved instruction is your most precious challenge.

Like it or not, the measurement of learning is usually achieved through testing, and this condition is not likely to go away anytime soon. Therefore, what the tests actually measure is especially significant in evaluating your child's progress or abilities. The testing activity itself does not need to be abandoned, but the content and presentation of test items does require continued scrutiny. Your visual-spatial child, like Syd, may be at a disadvantage if the test items do not measure spatial ability or visual knowledge in mathematics.

This section is an attempt to pave a path from OMG to Org. by outlining some of the stumbling blocks that your visual child might be facing. The three chapters in this Organization section are intended to begin the conversation around what confronts nonlinear thinkers in a math class. The organization around measuring with testing what your child knows, assessing what your child "sees" as it is reflected on the tests, and how to "redirect" your child's thinking in preparation for the test items are the issues in these three chapters.

The first chapter in this section describes some current assessments and how they measure, or don't measure, visual abilities referencing some of the subtests in the Wechsler series. The second chapter discusses what your child may actually see, or not see, during the learning process. The third chapter focuses on how you can help your child think differently about the mathematical pieces of information using the notion of a jigsaw puzzle organizational element to solve math problems.

NOTE

1. http://www.goodreads.com/quotes/6964233-sometimes-the-most-brilliant-and-intelligent-minds-do-not-shine.

Chapter 4

Assessments and the Visual-Spatial Child

Tests [must] measure what is of value, not just what is easy to test. If we want students to investigate, explore, and discover, assessments must not measure just mimicry mathematics.[1] —*Everybody Counts*

Your child may be smarter than the tests show. If your child is a spatial-mechanical learner and is only being tested on step-by-step computational tests, then their strengths cannot show up on these tests. Anyone "with particularly strong spatial abilities can go unrecognized through these traditional [test] means"[2] is a quote from a 2010 article in *Scientific American*. This article and Silverman's research speak to this testing issue, that "popular standardized tests used today do not adequately measure this [visual-spatial] trait."[3] Gardner joins the chorus by suggesting that standardized tests do not measure a child's full spectrum of abilities.

If your child scores high on math concepts and math comprehension sections and low on math computations, then that *could* indicate that you have a visual learner. According to Silverman and others, visual-spatial learners are better with the whole picture/context behind the concepts and not necessarily good with the details. The big picture for mathematics is in the Big Ideas of concepts like relationships, patterns, and connections; the details of number combinations are in the calculations. As the *Everybody Counts* document proclaims, tests need to measure what is of value, not mimicry math that only simulates the math.

Since the Russians launched Sputnik in the 1950s, generations of children have lived through, or in some cases suffered through, many standardized tests to measure the progress of their math learning. All of these tests seem to self-perpetuate, each trying to show the "real" gain or loss, and some even compare math progress across countries, curricula, and cultures. The test results that seem to catch the most media attention are the ones from the international math and science tests.

The 1990s Trends in International Mathematics and Science Study (TIMSS was recently changed from Third) was preceded by the First International Mathematics and Science Study (FIMSS) in the 1960s and the Second International Mathematics and

Science Study (SIMSS) in the early 1980s. Each time new tests are administered and results published, there is outcry and disdain about how poorly students are scoring.

Many rationales support the continuation of international tests and, of course, there are local tests also trying to help improve mathematics instruction. Unless these tests include a sufficient amount of visual-spatial test items, how can they adequately assess your visual child's progress? In more personal terms, what kinds of test items or instruction can actually measure your visual-spatial child's mathematics knowledge and problem-solving abilities? Standardized tests rely on sequentially printed words, so solutions to this issue are not simplistic. However, this question does need to be continually addressed by test developers.

The developers of the *Mathematics Diagnostic and Prescriptive Inventory* (MDPI) responded to the visual math assessment issue by developing an instrument that gathers information about children's thinking through evaluator observations while the child uses objects, pictures, and abstract symbols to think about and solve problems. The evaluation process includes a variety of questions allowing a global processor/visual-spatial learner to demonstrate their math skills and problem-solving abilities *their way*.

The Wechsler series of intelligence tests are generally used for diagnosing learning issues. The age of your child will determine which test is used: Wechsler Preschool and Primary Scale (WPPS) or the Wechsler Intelligence Tests for Children (WISC). Children over sixteen and adults take the Wechsler Intelligence Tests for Adults (WAIS). Lucile Beckman, Alexander Bannatyne, Alan Kaufman, and Linda Silverman have independently determined which of the subtests in these tests are indicators of spatial abilities.

VISUAL-SPATIAL AND TESTING

Researchers seem to agree that high scores for the Wechsler subtests for Block Design, Picture Arrangement, and Object Assembly indicate spatial strengths, especially if combined with low scores on the verbal-sequential subtests. However, these tests are not the only way to identify your child's spatial strengths. You can observe and take specific notice over time of what your child does well—builds things, shows creativity with projects, remembers visual details that surprise you, draws well, or responds better to showing rather than telling. These are some indicators that help you understand how your child can be smart, just in different ways.

Visual-spatial children don't learn in the same way as auditory-sequential children do, nor do they have the same methods to express their knowledge as the other children do. Clearly, they will not remember the same way. Visual children, and adults, can remember faces but not names. They need time to think about whatever the topic is, and they probably will not remember anything unless it fits into a larger idea that they have created in their imaginations or mental images. For visual children, memory depends on context.

You are your child's most important advocate and cheerleader. Identifying your child's strengths is your joy and your responsibility. Having that joy reach into mathematics learning can be daunting if you have not experienced any enjoyment in mathematics yourself. Maybe you are a spatial learner who never had the chance to show what you understood in math because the details, frustration, and missing-the-big-picture got in your way.

Testing is an integral part of school math lessons and curricula to measure progress and, hopefully, understanding. Testing and other assessments will probably not, nor should they, go away (okay, maybe not have so many of them). Just as your child can ask questions and analyze poetry for better understanding *before any of the tests*, your child can ask questions, make thoughtful guesses, sketch pictures *of their interpretations* of the math, trace, fold, imagine new ideas, and even stumble in math so that they can learn, and fix, what doesn't work. Stumbling and fixing are good for learning mathematics and need to happen *before* the test date.

SHOW YOUR WORK

"Show your work" can be a downfall of any math student taking a test, but especially so for the visual-spatial learner who is not good at "proof" details or showing the steps that they used. This is because they probably didn't use steps; they jumped to a creative, accurate conclusion. It is important for your child to know that there is a way to explain thinking that does not use sequential steps. Even if your child had a burst of intuition and just *knew* the answer, then their task, with your help, is to reverse-engineer their intuitive blast through some scaffolding and supportive questions like, "What if you tried _(name an option)_, what might have happened?"

Other supporting strategies that can help your child learn how to reverse-engineer their thinking are drawing or sketching pictures, free writing and journaling, and filling in blanks in puzzles or sentences. One reliable strategy that works well is to show your child the answer along with the problem statement so that your child can fill in the space with what *could* have been the igniter for their intuitive blast. These strategies should be used *before* any testing so that by the time the test comes around, your child can "show their work" to satisfy the evaluator.

Drawing or sketching works nicely to solve those word problems that sometimes confound Math Avoiders. Free writing or math journaling allows your child to express their thoughts in a judgment-free zone. Writing about what *could have been* that intuitive blast igniter could happen by trying to imagine what Roger von Oech would call the second-best answer or solution. The more your child draws, writes, imagines, and ignites, the better your child will be able to explain their thinking.

"Memory is intelligence-specific."[4] More practice or more study time does not guarantee remembering for a spatial learner—or any learner. They may be able to complete tomorrow's test, but what about the day after? Encouraging your child to *think* about math visually with some imagination is more dependable and, in the long run, is more effective. As your child writes about mathematics, they will usually make some connections of their own, especially if they are like Stephanie who wrote about her experience on the About Math card shown in Figure 4.1. Writing can help Stephanie, and your child too, to solidify their math thinking.

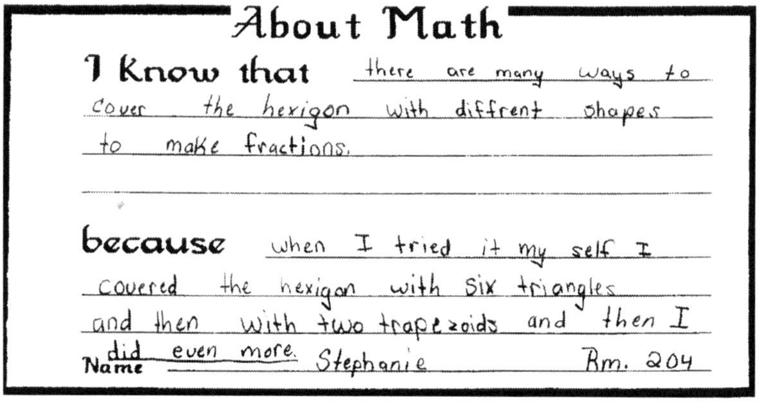

About Math

I Know that there are many ways to cover the hexigon with diffrent shapes to make fractions.

because when I tried it my self I covered the hexigon with six triangles and then with two trapezoids and then I did even more.

Name _Stephanie_ Rm. 204

Figure 4.1 Stephanie's description.

The "Who Am I?" cards in Figure 4.2 can help your visual child get involved in writing through some creative descriptions of math concepts or numbers, especially when they can get used to the idea by first filling in the blanks in partial sentences. These cards are similar to the "Think of a Number" puzzles in chapter 1 because they allow your child to imagine the number in their mind's eye and think about how to describe it with clues. The "Think of a Number" puzzles helped your child see the math relationships with objects and transfer the relationships to words and symbols. Both are ways to help your child "see" and communicate math relationships.

Who Am I?

I am a positive fraction.

My decimal has all 6's.

I am a ratio and I am less than 1.

Who Am I?

Who Am I?

My square root continues but does not have a pattern.

I am a multiple of 3 and less than 10.

I am an even integer.

Who Am I?

Who Am I?

I am a _____

I have a _____ as a factor.

I am a _____ less than _____.

Who Am I?

Who Am I?

My fact family has _____.

I am an _____ number.

I _____ a prime number.

Who Am I?

Figure 4.2

Math Avoiders, along with other learners, usually worry that they will be "found out" on these tests; everybody will know that they didn't study long enough, didn't work hard enough, or didn't do all the homework. The assumption is that if they had studied *harder* and longer, worked more, and done all the homework then of course they would get good grades, right? Not exactly. More study in the same way that hasn't worked is not a cure. Harder thinking is not a cure; they are already thinking *very hard* trying to climb over that Mount Visual Translation.

KEEP IN MIND

Different practice, *different* study, and *different* thinking will empower your child and *are* the components for curing a math confusion malady. Helping your child to think and describe math problems using metaphors, analogies, or similes will enable them to think about math differently. Your child's test scores *will* rise when they are able to problem-solve any given mathematical situation using their imagination. Your visual-learning child's test scores *will not* improve if they only practice and memorize rules. To problem-solve any mathematical situation means that your child will need to be flexible in their thinking.

NOTES

1. *Everybody Counts*, 1989, 70.
2. Park, *Recognizing Spatial Ability*, 3.
3. Park, *Spatial Ability and STEM*, 3.
4. Armstrong, *Multiple Intelligences in the Classroom*, 147.

Chapter 5

What You See Is What You Say

Wow, this is easy when you know what to look for. —student in college-level
Basic Algebra course

Your child *cannot* see or say what they cannot *see*. If they cannot see, then they do
not know what is missing either. This "seeing" can be a physical eyesight problem, a
visual processing difficulty, or an inability to recognize the math. The college Basic
Algebra student had just discovered a missing piece of information that had eluded
him for years. This chapter is about how your child can miss information because of
three issues related to seeing—eyesight problems that a good pair of glasses will help,
visual processing issues that need to be identified, and mental "seeing" that a good
imagination can inspire.

Most of the students in that particular remedial Basic Algebra class had previously
known little success with mathematics but now experienced the excitement of discovery because the instruction in that algebra class incorporated visual-spatial methods.
The math patterns and relationships now made sense to them because they could "see"
them. Knowing *what* to look for, what it was *supposed* to look like, and *how* to look
for it were world-opening math events for the Math Avoiders in that classroom. They
had never known what they were supposed to see, much less do, because the missing
pieces had been hidden from their mental views.

EYESIGHT THAT A GOOD PAIR OF GLASSES WILL HELP

The three images in Figure 5.1 show examples of some eyesight difficulties. A good
pair of eyeglasses could probably make the first and second images clearer. The third
image could represent what a child doesn't "see" in the details of the vertical letters, a
visual perception problem. Although many Math Avoiders with no eyesight or visual
perception problems frequently exclaim that the scribbles in the third image are what
math looks like to them all of the time, this is a translation or an interpretation problem
and not an eyesight issue.

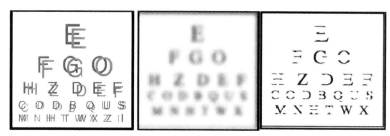

Figure 5.1

Your child might be reasonably asking, "Where am I supposed to be looking?" or "What am I *supposed* to see?" when working with math concepts. These two questions are commonly expressed through the statement, "I don't get it." which is fourth grade, or any grade, code for *please explain again*.[1] Logically, if your child *can't* see it, then what they say is unclear, and they cannot mentally *see* it either. Whether your child has fuzzy or double-vision eyesight problems or difficulties with visual perceptions, these conditions need to be diagnosed *before* trying any visual-spatial or creative explanations.

No amount of repeated, louder, or even intricately devised step-by-step verbal directions can fix these predicaments, but a regular eye exam with an optometrist or a visual developmental optometrist can. As for those mental images created by visual learners, those imaginative creations are far more interesting than math symbols, so when trying your explanations of mathematical ideas and concepts, be sure to capitalize on your child's already rich "minds eye" or visual imagination.

EYESIGHT THAT MAY NEED MORE THAN A GOOD PAIR OF EYEGLASSES

A video entitled "How Difficult Can This Be?"[2] featuring instructor Richard Lavoie shows some typical scenarios that visually challenged students must endure in classrooms. Several adults and one student attend the mock classroom setting in the video. Some of the participants are parents, some are teachers, and some are interested people from the community. Only the student has one or more of the specific visual disabilities described in the video program. The purpose of Lavoie's mock classroom is to simulate a classroom circumstance when a child might experience the trauma of having these difficulties.

A developmental optometrist can provide a good diagnosis and remediation exercises to reduce visual eyesight and processing challenges. Communication with your child's teacher and other adults involved in your child's learning experiences provides the information needed to monitor your child's visual health. The following seven visual skill descriptions can affect the success of learning mathematical symbolism and concepts. Some are developmental in nature and can be outgrown; some are not and need to be addressed.

Two of the seven visual processing skill difficulties that can interfere with math learning are associated with making comparisons necessary for classifying, constructing, and ordering sequences: Visual Discrimination and Spatial Relationships. Visual Discrimination allows your child to identify similarities and differences in order to sort and classify objects. Having a good sense for Spatial Relationships allows your child to see two or more objects in relation to each other as in building towers or structures and building patterns.

Two visual processing skills affect your child's ability to recognize and accept congruence of shapes and equality of numbers, regardless of position or location or arrangement: Position in Space Perception and Perceptual Constancy. Position in Space Perception allows your child to understand "left" and "right" and other positions. Space Perception also allows your child to sequence items, such as small to large or high to low. A difficulty in space perception with symbols can show up in *temporary* reversals of symbols. Perceptual Constancy allows your child to recognize that "the same" does not depend on location.

Three visual processing skills permit your child to improvise, understand, and try different perspectives: Visual Closure, Figure Ground Discrimination, and Construction of Images. Visual Closure is present when your child does not need every little detail to interpret meaning and can mentally fill in reasonable missing elements to make sense of what they *do* see. Figure Ground Discrimination allows your child to visually "pull out" images from surrounding information such as recognizing similar triangles in a painting's vanishing point. Construction of Images allows your child to "see" an object from several perspectives.

One visual difficulty that a young child might outgrow is the reversal of some digits and letters. If your child does not outgrow these reversals, then a good diagnostician can test your child for dyslexia, a condition that affects the way the brain processes information. "Dyslexics themselves are frequently endowed with high talents in many areas."[3] Usually these children can understand complex concepts, but just cannot deal with those small symbols. Using strategies that do not initially require those small details of the symbol reversals will help both you and your child avoid the frustrations in translating those mathematical symbols.

MENTAL SIGHT THAT A GOOD IMAGINATION CAN HELP

Mathematics can be so saturated with symbols and technical details that the overall ideas are lost in the shuffle, especially if your child cannot "see" or translate all or any of the details. Math is about the collection and the relationships between and among the symbols, not the symbols themselves. An inundation with details can stifle a visual learner, resulting in a kind of "clutter blindness," unless there are some Big Ideas or larger concepts where the details can fit. The math relationships were there first, followed by the symbolism. The details of symbolism and formulas describing these relationships are everywhere in math, and are unavoidable.

Limiting your child's mathematics experiences to the grinding of formulas does not encourage your child to see mathematics with their own eyes because those formulas were developed by and through other people's eyes. Using only formulas does not let your child make the mistakes, develop the patterns, generalize the patterns, and experience the joy of "seeing and therefore believing." When formulas are presented as an *experience* of the relationships, your child will be able to learn what to look for, communicate the relationships that they "see in their own way," and eventually translate the relationships to symbols.

HOW TO CAPITALIZE ON WHAT YOUR CHILD DOES SEE

Your child *can* describe how and what they are thinking, just very possibly not in the way that you expect. You may not understand your child's pictures, but those pictures do come with reasonable explanations when viewed through the eyes of the beholder. Your child needs permission to think differently and a safe place to try some alternate explanations of their ideas. Some children write stories about the ideas, some draw diagrams or pictures, and others describe the math in their mind's eye with metaphors, analogies, or paradoxes. The road from mental image to math symbol is not a straight path, and it clearly isn't precise in its early stages.

The more your child traces, folds, moves, and rotates, the better they are able to translate their thinking from ideas to results. Trying to create or "compose" a picture or take apart or "decompose" a picture will give your child some "sweat equity" in exploring what makes a diagram worth studying. For example, the square inscribed in the circle in Figure 5.2 was created by folding a round coffee filter into four equal sections and then drawing a line across the circumference edge from one corner of the section to the other on all of the quarter sections. A right triangle is in that one-quarter fold.

Figure 5.2   Folding a coffee filter.

Diagrams in math problems are supposed to help see relationships but because of the particular arrangement in the diagram, your child might be like Charles, a high-school student who did not recognize the individual pieces. After Charles disassembled and rearranged the picture in Figure 5.3, he described the diagram as being "like overlays in different sections that can change" so that it "gives you more choices." If your child is like Charles, the right triangle in the math diagram doesn't look like a right triangle because it is not in the usual orientation. Your child, and Charles, may not know that they have the option of rearranging it so that it does.

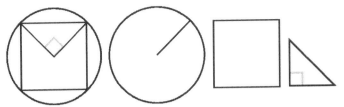

Figure 5.3   Charlie's separated parts of the diagram.

Your child can trace the right triangle on tracing paper, lift the tracing paper off the diagram, and then turn it until it looks like a right triangle. Like Charles, your child may need "permission" to rearrange the picture because to them, math is static and fixed on the paper. Charles, a visual learner, had the ability to visualize math arrangements, but the pieces in the diagram were bolted together. He had never been given "permission" to rearrange or reassemble math diagrams. For him, the lines, angles, and shapes within shapes were fixed, immovable, and therefore unavailable to alternate solutions.

Charles' attempts to use the typical problem-solving strategies on unmovable pieces caused many of his "careless errors." These errors turned out to not be careless at all but carefully thought through, yet mathematically inappropriate, strategies. After he had permission to separate pieces *and* move them around to his own advantage in order to recognize mathematically appropriate relationships, his solutions to math problems became reliable and his math scores improved!

Another way to help your child develop their mental imaging skills is to use a sock box like the one shown in Figure 5.4. A sock box is made with a plastic container pushed into a sock that may have seen better days or lost its other pair. Different items are placed in the sock box so that your child can reach in, feel the items, and then use their imagination to describe the items. The purpose of the sock box is to engage your child's imagination and to help them identify what Math Aficionados call properties. Your child can use their *own* words to describe properties of items or, like second grader Shelly, may prefer to draw the item rather than use written words.

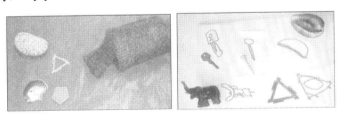

Figure 5.4   Sock box and contents.

Never say, tell, or describe anything that your child could observe, identify, or explain with their words. Provide the opportunity for them to talk, describe, draw, and ask questions. When children start to use descriptions, they are beginning to identify properties. Think of adjectives as early onset properties. It's easy to assume that your child will "see" your pictures representing a mathematical relationship and understand them the same way that you do. This isn't necessarily true and besides, your child is much more interested in *their* pictures.

A DIFFERENT WAY TO SEE MATH "FACTS"

Drilling the math "facts" is a rite of passage in elementary schools; however, cutting out sections and comparing math "facts" may be a helpful and divergent activity. You might use an addition math facts chart and cut it into two stair-step pieces like the one shown in Figure 5.5. The dark lines show the cut lines; the diagonal with the even numbers is excluded. Compare the numbers in the cutout sections. Take turns to describe any number relationships and patterns in the cutouts. If your child sees a relationship *and* can describe it, then what they say is acceptable. The same activity works with a multiplication table. Don't drill; investigate patterns instead.

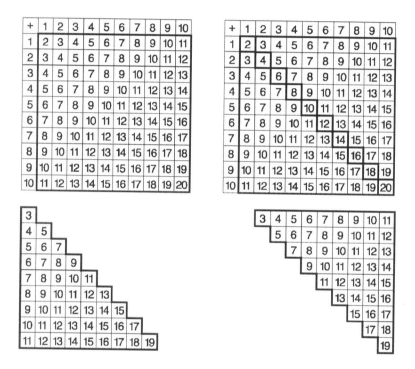

Figure 5.5   Addition cutouts.

Although subtraction tables are not part of the elementary curriculum, they provide a good source for an investigation. Addition tables and multiplication tables have matching "puzzle" stair-step cutouts; however, the subtraction table cutouts in Figure 5.6 do *not* have matching numbers in the same way. The numbers in the subtraction table cutouts do not match in the same way, but they do have a relationship. Pair the numbers as you would for a subtraction problem to equal zero. The numbers that pair this way are called "additive inverses of each other" because they match in pairs to add to each other to get the zero on the diagonal.

a-b		a									
		1	2	3	4	5	6	7	8	9	10
b	1	0	1	2	3	4	5	6	7	8	9
	2	-1	0	1	2	3	4	5	6	7	8
	3	-2	-1	0	1	2	3	4	5	6	7
	4	-3	-2	-1	0	1	2	3	4	5	6
	5	-4	-3	-2	-1	0	1	2	3	4	5
	6	-5	-4	-3	-2	-1	0	1	2	3	4
	7	-6	-5	-4	-3	-2	-1	0	1	2	3
	8	-7	-6	-5	-4	-3	-2	-1	0	1	2
	9	-8	-7	-6	-5	-4	-3	-2	-1	0	1
	10	-9	-8	-7	-6	-5	-4	-3	-2	-1	0

a-b		a									
		1	2	3	4	5	6	7	8	9	10
b	1	0	1	2	3	4	5	6	7	8	9
	2	-1	0	1	2	3	4	5	6	7	8
	3	-2	-1	0	1	2	3	4	5	6	7
	4	-3	-2	-1	0	1	2	3	4	5	6
	5	-4	-3	-2	-1	0	1	2	3	4	5
	6	-5	-4	-3	-2	-1	0	1	2	3	4
	7	-6	-5	-4	-3	-2	-1	0	1	2	3
	8	-7	-6	-5	-4	-3	-2	-1	0	1	2
	9	-8	-7	-6	-5	-4	-3	-2	-1	0	1
	10	-9	-8	-7	-6	-5	-4	-3	-2	-1	0

Figuure 5.6   Subtraction cutouts.

SEEING FRACTIONS WITH PICTURES—OR NOT

Pictures are usually part of the early introduction of fractions but can be as much of a hindrance as they are helpful, depending on what your child sees in the pictures. Helen, an adult student, was able to articulate her confusion. Her confusion *was* the picture because she did not even "see" the division as part of the explanation, nor did she "see" that extra black line that usually marks the rest of the whole. Figure 5.7 shows what Helen saw and possibly what other quiet students might see but do not tell anyone. In Helen's case, the problem was neither a physical eyesight nor a visual processing difficulty.

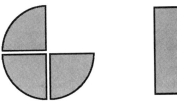 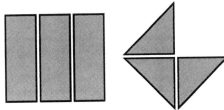

Figure 5.7   What Helen saw.

Helen's problem was similar to Charles' problem; both involved difficulties with the pieces. Charles couldn't separate the pieces and Helen didn't know which *pieces* of the picture were useful. Helen never knew that she had to consider that extra black line around the perimeter that delineated the "whole" part of the fraction picture in Figure 5.8. Even though she could literally see the black line in the picture on the page, she had never understood *how* the line was useful or even significant. Helen never knew that she needed to consider it *ever* because she never asked. Helen, Charles, and possibly your child too, thought that the picture was rigid.

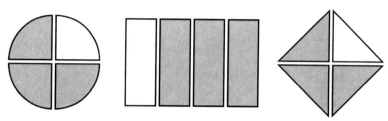

Figure 5.8   What was on the page.

These pictures of fractions were useless to Helen, even confounding to her, but when given a blank circle, long rectangle, and square to slice each evenly to share with four people, *she* recognized the fraction pieces because *she* sliced them. The key was allowing her to do the cutting and sharing herself. Helen was a visual learner with a need for hands-on understanding. All of the previous auditory-sequential instruction had not been very helpful. As a parent, if you know about this division relationship for fractions, you can be more sensitive and helpful to your child. Helen's understanding came through a pair of scissors.

Sectioned circles, rectangles, and squares are not the only pictures used for fractions that can confuse your child. The three pictures for fractions shown in Figure 5.9 have the same circle and the same number of sections, only the number of dots is different. These three circles looked very different to Dave, a Math Avoider. The shaded circles, rectangles, and squares along with the circles with dots are strikingly different pictures to the Math Avoider. Dave's reasoning: How can different pictures show the same fraction ratio? Math Aficionados likely recognize common multiples in the pictures. Math Avoiders start screaming!

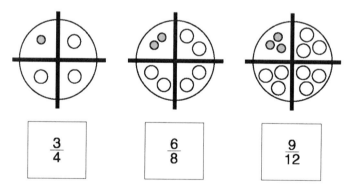

Figure 5.9

The number of sections in the pictures in Figure 5.9 is the clue to the pattern equivalence. The relationship illustrated by all of the dots inside the circles remains the same because the number of sections stays the same. The number of sections controls the relationship equivalence. The black dots and the total dots increase by the same multiple. A round coffee filter can come to the rescue again for those struggling with these flat pictures. Replace the dots with color chips or disks after your child folds the coffee filter into the four sections. Fractions with a different denominator, like 3 or 5, will fold differently but will still keep both colors of chips.

Look for the connection between the number of sections, both shaded and not shaded, in each of the shapes in Figure 5.10. All three shapes have four sections and only three sections are shaded. Here is an example of when a number needs to be "freed" from the specifics of the picture. Typically, the shaded regions are treated as the parts and the total number of sections is the whole. However, your child might choose to consider the clear piece as the part and all of the sections as the whole. Just know that your child must be consistent and keep the sections the same size. When you change the shading reference, you change the fraction relationship.

Three shaded pieces out of four total pieces or $\frac{3}{4}$

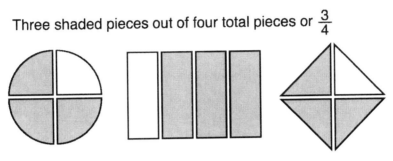

Figure 5.10

Another confusion can occur when you tell your child to count the whole amount and the part amount and then write both numbers for a fraction. Your child might be thinking that you are changing the rules about counting and suggesting that *now* it is okay to count some of the items twice, remembering their earlier counting experiences when they got in trouble when they counted things twice. Your child will need an explanation that will help them figure out when they have "permission" to count twice and when they don't. This idea for "reassembly of the part back into a whole amount" needs special attention when learning about fractions.

At this stage, Math Avoiders are dealing with many moving parts, strange double-counting interpretations, and many different-looking pictures. To a Math Avoider, if the picture changes from a circle to a rectangle to a square, then the fraction should change. They are looking at the shape and not at the count. They don't understand that the fraction ratio is in the count and not in the shape. The number relationship needs its freedom from the images. Reduce the number of moving parts for the Math Avoider, and anyone else, by focusing on only one similarity at a time. Look for similarities across the shape images; look for the same *counts*.

The shaded parts compared with the total shape parts in Figure 5.11 are similar to the number of color dots compared with the total dots in the circles. The visual learner has already noticed that the circle and the square have two cuts, while the rectangle has only one cut, yet the same number is assigned to all of the three images. This kind of variation needs discussion because the visual clues appear to be deceiving. Numbers freed from the shapes allows your child to count the number of parts despite the shape differences and cuts. Don't let the picture get in the way. Let your child's fingers do the counting and let go of the shapes.

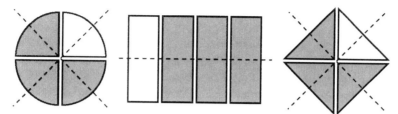

Figure 5.11

The comparison of the shaded pieces with the total in each image in Figure 5.12 shows that all of the images have 6/8 of the whole shaded. The shape outlines no longer matter when looking at the similarities of the number relationships. Since we started with 3/4 and did not change the "whole" in each case, then the 3/4 = 6/8; the only change is in the number of pieces. Cutting or dividing the shapes can continue in order to provide more sections and more equivalent fractions. *How* your child chooses to cut or fold is their choice, but your child *must* maintain equal *sections* with each cut or fold.

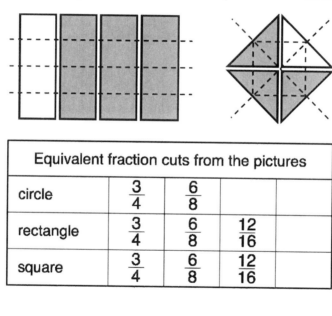

Equivalent fraction cuts from the pictures			
circle	$\frac{3}{4}$	$\frac{6}{8}$	
rectangle	$\frac{3}{4}$	$\frac{6}{8}$	$\frac{12}{16}$
square	$\frac{3}{4}$	$\frac{6}{8}$	$\frac{12}{16}$

$\frac{3}{4}$	$\frac{6}{8}$	$\frac{9}{12}$	$\frac{12}{16}$	$\frac{15}{20}$	$\frac{18}{24}$	$\frac{21}{28}$	$\frac{24}{32}$	$\frac{27}{36}$	$\frac{30}{40}$	$\frac{33}{44}$	$\frac{36}{48}$

Figure 5.12

Compare the fraction strip in Figure 5.12 with equivalent fractions for these fraction cuts for the shapes. Look for common characteristics among the numbers in both the numerator and the denominator and *then* look at the overall ratio. Does the fraction strip have equivalent fractions that the shapes do not show with the cuts? Do you think you could cut the shapes to generate all of the fractions in the pattern from the fraction strip?

KEEP IN MIND

For the visual-spatial learner, seeing is everything, not just a perk. Seeing in their mind's eye and literally seeing by eyesight are their gateways for understanding the relationships in mathematics. Syd, Helen, and Charles, and your child too, all need opportunities to share their math ideas in any way that makes sense to them *and* to mathematical thinking. Those two mountains are still there to climb, Mount Visual Translation and Mount Slow-At-Math.

NOTES

1. Kinnan, "Communication Speaks," 28.
2. Lavoie, *How Difficult Can This Be?*, https://www.youtube.com/watch?v=zHQA3u-KPXc.
3. West, *In the Mind's Eye*, 34.

Chapter 6

Finding Your Math Jigsaw Strengths

The real voyage of discovery consists not in seeking new landscapes but in having new eyes.[1] —Marcel Proust

Visual-spatial learners can use their imagination and intuition to assemble the puzzle pieces of a newly introduced math topic if they know the overall idea of how the pieces might fit together. The cover picture on a jigsaw puzzle box serves that purpose for puzzle solvers. If your child can see the "picture on the cover of the math puzzle," then they have an end goal to work toward. If your child knows that there *is* an overall concept, like a jigsaw puzzle box cover, for the math that they are learning, then their efforts have purpose.

In general, jigsaw puzzle fanciers tend to fall into one of two categories: those who work from the edges in, putting together the edges first, and those who work from the inner pieces first by sorting the shapes and colors and then building outward. Either way, there is an initial classification and a strategy for working that provides the puzzle solver with the satisfying confirmation of the final assembled result. Your child can find their best strategy in solving the "math thinking puzzles" if they know that that there *is* an overall Big Idea concept when all of the math pieces fit together and make sense.

Multiplication is a math topic that lends itself to a Big Idea for organizing pieces with a "puzzle box cover image" of rectangle blocks. The rectangle box cover arrangement itself is not the full concept, but it does provide a general organization for the numbers to fit into a "puzzle box cover image" for multiplication. Your child does not need to formally know about the area concept because the math arrangement depends only on counting and assembling the different-sized blocks. Larger blocks require more regrouping and therefore lead into higher grade levels.

MULTIPLY WITH BASE TEN BLOCKS JIGSAW

Think of the jigsaw picture in Figure 6.1 as the cover of the math jigsaw box. The cover image shows a two-digit multiplication problem for 45 × 53 and the related rectangle block arrangement diagram. The cover on this math jigsaw box provides a peek at a connection between the multiplication procedure from third or fourth grade math class and the organizational arrangement of the blocks that "explains" the placement of the digits in the procedure. The outside perimeter edges of the "box cover" provide the clues to the two numbers in the problem. The 45 is from the top edge and the 53 is alongside the adjacent side edge.

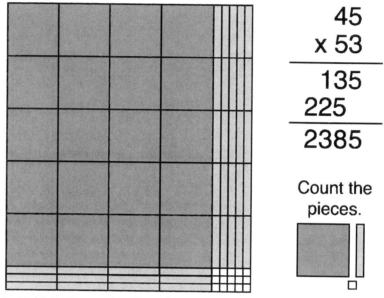

$$\begin{array}{r} 45 \\ \times\ 53 \\ \hline 135 \\ 225 \\ \hline 2385 \end{array}$$

Count the pieces.

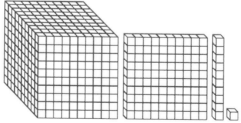

Figure 6.1   Multiplication problem jigsaw box cover.

A refresher for the base ten block shapes is in Figure 6.2, which shows the largest to smallest blocks from left-to-right: thousand block, hundred block, ten block, and the one block. Using these rectangular blocks *will* fit *all* multiplication problems but is only one way to show multiplication. As one parent said, "This really *is* math. I thought it was just pictures." The multiplication problem in Figure 6.1 requires regrouping ("carrying and borrowing" to the 1950s crowd, "trading" for the 1960s crowd, "regrouping" for the 1980s crowd, and "composing or decomposing" for the children of the new millennium), so it will need some "translations."

Figure 6.2   Base ten blocks.

The translation of the rectangular pieces on the math jigsaw puzzle box cover to the multiplication of the two two-digit numbers happens by using the hundred, ten, and one blocks from the set of base ten blocks used during the first and second grade place value organization days. The multiplication arrangement also works with bags of items like golf tees, buttons, or sticks but not until after the bagged items have been converted to two-digit place value notation. The bagged items may not be as easy to recognize as the blocks to show an arrangement.

Only the two-dimensional faces of the blocks are used in the jigsaw math puzzle pieces just as the jigsaw pieces in regular puzzles represent only the two-dimensional picture of the puzzle scene. Our math puzzle initially uses only hundred, ten, and one unit blocks; however, the thousand block appears when the regrouping happens during the final stage. The ten thousand and hundred thousand blocks can be made into a jigsaw puzzle, too, because the *ten thousand* block will look like a *very* large ten block and the *hundred thousand* block will be a *very* large hundred block. This puzzle would make a *very, very* large three-dimensional one.

EARLY STAGES FOR SMALLER PUZZLES

In the second or third grade, your child will work only with the circled blocks in Figure 6.3 in the lower right corner that show fifteen small unit cubes. In the third and fourth grades, they will learn how to regroup fifteen small cubes into one ten and five ones or group the thirty-seven "ten" sticks into three hundreds with seven extra ten sticks. In the fourth or fifth grade, the twenty hundred-block squares encircled with a dotted line on the left side of the diagram are regrouped into two thousand-sized cubes. These different stages are shown in Figure 6.3 by circling the hundred-block squares and the one-block squares separately from the long ten blocks.

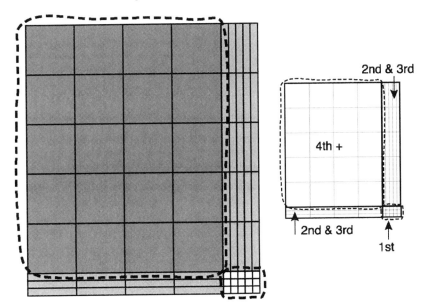

Figure 6.3

When multiplication is in the beginning stages of the first, second, or third grade, your child will probably group and regroup several different kinds of objects. Some of those objects will be small squares or cubes like the pieces in this math jigsaw puzzle. The arrangement in these early grades will use only the ones cubes or pictures of squares and will look like the cubes in Figure 6.4 that evolve in abstraction levels from cubes to squares to a rectangular outline. That 3 × 5 outline looks like an enlargement of the one squares from the lower right corner of the math jigsaw puzzle cover in Figure 6.1.

Figure 6.4

After the initial introduction stages, your child will regroup and trade the one blocks into the ten blocks. Some children learn to regroup or trade earlier than third grade; however, by fourth grade, your child will be well into the regrouping process. The two-digit arrangements from the math jigsaw puzzle initially use the tens blocks and the ones blocks beginning with five groups of one ten and three ones, as represented in Figure 6.5, as five rows of thirteen blocks, or 5 × 15. Later, all five of the long ten blocks from the right side of the cover image will make the more complicated problem of five groups of five tens and three ones, or 5 × 53.

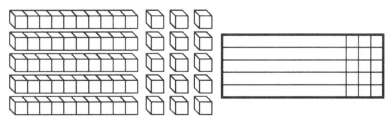

Figure 6.5

The arrangement and regrouping process continues using larger blocks for larger numbers. When your child recognizes that all of these multiplication problems are simply arrangements of blocks, then the mystery behind "where to put the numbers" becomes a matter of placing the digits where they can describe the number of blocks. By the time your child reaches the two-digit multiplication problems that require multiple trades, the problems will look like the original jigsaw math puzzle.

FINAL ASSEMBLY OF THE TWO-DIGIT JIGSAW PUZZLE

The outside-in strategists sort the pieces of this math jigsaw puzzle by putting the edge pieces together first and then filling in with the inner pieces. Since all of the puzzle pieces have straight edges, the outside-in fanciers will need to use the picture to make decisions about which pieces belong on the outside edges and where they need to be placed. The inside-out fanciers will sort the pieces by shape or maybe by color.

The top sorting of pieces in Figure 6.6 shows the edge sort first with the other pieces to the side. The inside-out sorting strategy of grouping by shape and color is shown in the second grouping. Both groups have all of the puzzle pieces.

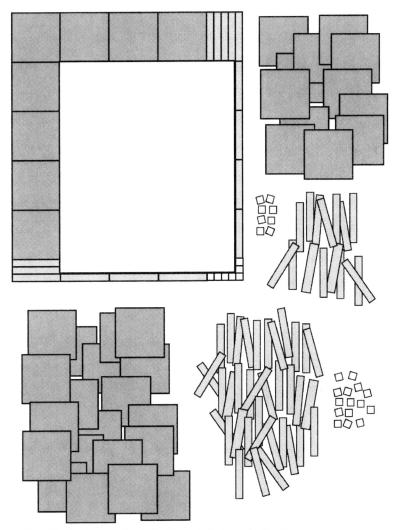

Figure 6.6 Outside-in strategy (top); Inside-out strategy (bottom).

When the jigsaw puzzle for 45 × 53 is assembled, the next stage for the math procedure is to translate the blocks to the numbers in the multiplication problem. All of the pieces in the puzzle are counted and reorganized (regrouped) so that the number digits describe the correct block. The fifteen ones in the lower right are traded in for one ten and five ones. The thirty-seven ten blocks are traded for three of the hundred-block squares and seven ten sticks. The twenty hundred-block squares are stacked and traded in for two of the thousand cubes that were not even on the jigsaw cover, but because of the trade-in, that thousand block must be counted.

Mathematical relationships may be visual, but the language of the math is eventually translated into symbols. That is the reason for place value organization, where the organization with base ten enters into the translation of the symbols as shown in Figure 6.7. Combine all blocks, swapping blocks to the next larger more compact unit every time you reach ten of any kind of block. The total number of blocks will end up being the same 2385 on the box cover!

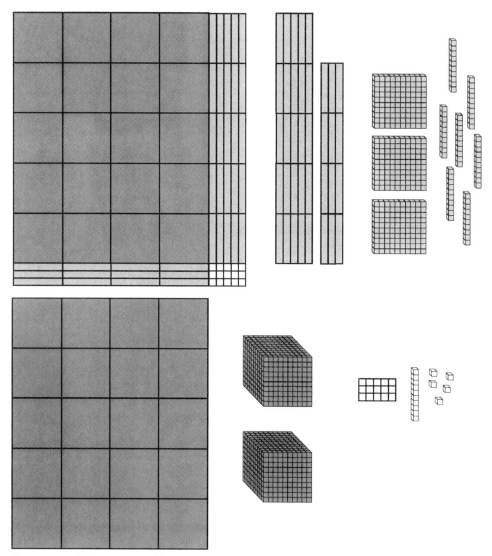

Figure 6.7   Final stage assembly.

This explanation might give you a feel for how confused your child could be if they are not encouraged to arrange the blocks, swap, trade, or otherwise regroup the blocks to show equivalent blocks all along the way. If your child gets only the put-the-digit-here-and-carry-the-tens-to-the-next-column treatment, then they have no place or general idea for this regrouping topic to fit. Your child's mental picture cannot be formed without their own interpretations and experimentations with the arrangements and rearrangements.

DIFFERENT MULTIPLICATION TABLE JIGSAWS

The cover on a different jigsaw puzzle box for the multiplication table looks like the top multiplication table in Figure 6.8 that has only rectangle puzzle pieces, squares included. Instead of the usual multiplication table with numbers, this 100-piece puzzle contains rectangle shapes that are multiples of the 1 × 1 corner square in the upper left corner. The outliner strategists will probably use the edges first like the second arrangement below the multiplication "box cover picture" top photo in Figure 6.8. The inside-out strategists might sort the blocks by the same shape pairs, squares, or rectangles with the same measures on one side.

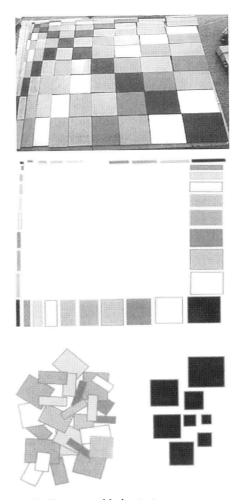

Figure 6.8   Multiplication table jigsaw outside-in strategy.

The blocks in this "shape multiplication table" intrigued a second grader named Jesse. Although she had already started multiplying with single-digit numbers, she did not pay attention to any numbers as she fit the blocks in the puzzle frame. When the blocks were spread out beside the multiplication table jigsaw frame, she decided to sort by size and then by color. Without instruction, Jesse started to notice several diagonal patterns as she figured out where to place the blocks. She also noticed that the blocks came in pairs and if one fit on one side, then the same shape size would also fit on the other side. Math Aficionados call this "the commutative property."

Two other versions of a multiplication table jigsaw puzzle use a combination of the numbers and shapes. Your child must cut out the shapes for both of these versions. The box covers for these multiplication table puzzles have a 9 × 9 multiplication table; however, a 10 × 10 multiplication grid or even a 12 × 12 grid will work. The larger the grid, the more shapes to cut out and the more relationships to see.

For the first version for the puzzle assembly, all of the numbers in the table are removed from the box cover, except the top and side numbers. Your child will make the puzzle pieces by cutting out the rectangle pieces that fit on the table. To put the puzzle together, place the shapes so that they fit on the grid always keeping one corner on the 1 × 1 square. The rectangles will overlap. Two sample pairs of rectangular pieces, shown in Figure 6.9, show one pair of rectangles with 20 squares and the other pair with 10 squares in each. Even though the rectangles have the same number of squares, the rectangles may look different, but they aren't. They are only rotated.

The puzzle is complete when all empty squares have a number and all rectangles are overlapped. Let your child "see" their own math beauty in their arrangements. Yes, all of the numbers in the multiplication table will have at least one rectangle; some numbers have two rectangles and some have three or four. The number of rectangles for any given number will depend on the size of the multiplication grid that is on the cover of the jigsaw multiplication table box.

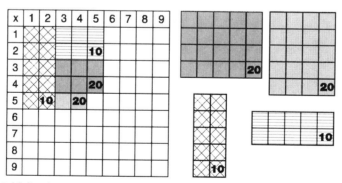

Figure 6.9   Multiplication area overlays 10s and 20s.

The second version uses the same cutout shapes, but this puzzle does not put the shapes on the multiplication grid. Instead, the rectangles with the same area are colored, stacked, and overlapped in separate groups. After your child cuts out all of the rectangle pieces for each of the numbers in the jigsaw multiplication table, they sort the rectangles by area and color all of the rectangles with the same area with the same color. Some of the stacks will have four rectangles and some stacks will have two rectangles, depending on the original size grid. There will be two rectangles with 20 squares for an area in the 9 × 9 grid. Look for a stack with only one rectangle.

Stack the rectangles with the same area and same color, all sharing one common corner. One of the examples in Figure 6.10 shows four overlay stacks of rectangles with 20 as the area that came from a 10 × 10 grid. The other example from the same 10 × 10 grid shows three stacked rectangles with an area of 36, including the 6 × 6 square. The pattern for the "20 area stack" in algebra is symbolized with $x \cdot y = 20$ because area is calculated with length times width. The algebra formula pattern for the "36 area stack" is $x \cdot y = 36$. Larger grids allow for more stacks and more rectangles. These stacks only show area arrangements with whole numbers.

Put dots on the outer corners of the overlays and connect the dots. The beginning of a curved graph begins to appear. As the multiplication grid grows to 12 × 12 or even higher, the number of rectangles increases and therefore there will be more dots to connect. From third grade, multiplication rectangles to algebra just happened in a flash of colors and overlays. So Charles was right after all; math patterns can appear as overlays.

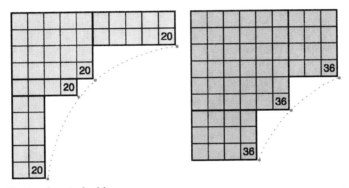

Figure 6.10   Rectangles stacked by same area.

WORD PROBLEM JIGSAWS

Word problem jigsaw puzzles may or may not have a cover picture to the box. Many word problems will require that your child create their own cover by drawing a picture of what the story is about. The strategies are the same, outside-in strategy and inside-out strategy. The outside-in strategists identify the boundaries for the story. The inside-out strategists find which parts of the story are the same or similar or are useful at all. An example of a word problem story associated with geometry is "A five-sided regular polygon has a perimeter of 60 units. What is the length of each side?"

A fifth grader named Jack drew the pentagon in Figure 6.11 as his box cover. He had difficulty until he realized that the pentagon has the same shape as home plate. After he recognized his home plate pentagon, he found out that "regular" meant that the sides of his pentagon had to be equal. What if the word problem changed? A revised pentagon word problem could be "A pentagon has a perimeter of 60 units. All sides are even numbers but none of the sides are equal to each other. What are the possible lengths of the sides?" The box cover changes and the pieces change. What pieces could be in the new word problem jigsaw box?[2]

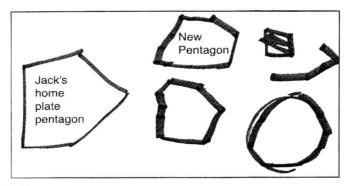

Figure 6.11   Jack's pentagons.

Test questions with phrases like "an odd number is three times another number" or "my aunt's age is six times my age" can send chills up the spine unless you are a Math Aficionado. These kinds of word problems can be treated like a jigsaw puzzle because your child can find the pieces just by writing one phrase piece at a time. The example word problem in Figure 6.12 shows how to write about one piece at a time, starting with the even numbers and then continuing with the odd numbers. Keep going until you reach the 13 needed to find the even number that is needed to answer the question.

"Four times an even number is 13 more than three times the next odd number." What is the even number?

List some even numbers	Multiply each by 4
2	4 x 2 = 8
4	4 x 4 = 16
6	4 x 6 = 24
8	4 x 8 = 32
10	4 x 10 = 40

Next, use the odd numbers that follow the even numbers.

Odd number	Multiply these odd numbers by three.
3	3 x 3 = 9
5	3 x 5 = 15
7	3 x 7 = 21
9	3 x 9 = 27
11	3 x 11 = 33

Subtract the pairs of even and odd multiplied numbers, toss if they do not equal 13.

Figure 6.12

Since your child is looking for an even number multiple that is already 13 more than the odd number multiple, your child needs to compare the two sets, one by one, and stop when the 13 is reached. Continue the numbers in the list in Figure 6.12 until you find the even number multiple that is 13 more than its partnered odd number multiple. That even number will be 16 and the odd number is 17. In an algebra class the even number is written as 2x and the comparison looks like an equation, $4(2x) = 3(2x + 1) + 13$. In the fourth grade, the comparison is about subtracting until the even-odd pair of multiplied numbers has the necessary 13 difference.

KEEP IN MIND

Avoid any circumstance that makes the jigsaw stop being a puzzle and turn into an assignment. Jigsaw puzzle thinking can help your child have new eyes to see any math problems *their way* as relationships with puzzle pieces. Your child learns that the pieces *do* fit together when they can find the pieces, just like with regular jigsaw puzzles. The intrigue of a jigsaw puzzle is generated by the search for and discovery of the pieces, the assembly of the pieces, and seeing the finished puzzle put together. Math jigsaw puzzles work this way, too. Remember, your child's jigsaw method is all about how *they* think and put the pieces together in *their* head.

NOTES

1. http://www.brainyquote.com/quotes/quotes/m/marcelprou107111.html.
2. Answer: Jack's new pentagon box could have several groups of pieces: one set could be 14, 12, 18, 10, 6 and another one could be 16, 10, 12, 2, 20. As long as the numbers are even and add up to 60, then they will work.

Part III

RELATIONSHIPS WITH MATHEMATICS

Be curious, not judgmental.[1] —Walt Whitman

The greatest deterrents to successful mathematics learning may be those well-intentioned, but hasty, judgments about wrong answers. Those hasty judgments can dampen your child's spirits beyond the point of even trying a second time. Your child's answer may not be totally wrong or it could be the mistake that redirects their thinking toward an alternate solution. Math Avoiders have learned to fear the mistakes and wrong answers, while Math Aficionados have learned to embrace and even expect them.

This Relationship section is about how a relationship with mathematics can affect your child: fear it, like it, or be inspired by it. The topics in these chapters give parents some positive options for helping their children to develop improved thinking strategies and therefore an improved relationship with mathematics. How a child evolves into a Math Avoider and how Math Aficionados work are the focus of the first two chapters, including what a Math Aficionado knows that a Math Avoider doesn't. The third chapter is all about the inside work of gaining insights by probing inside the math relationships and connections.

Chris had no patience for just manipulating the symbols in those seventh grade practice multiplication and division worksheets. Try as she might to memorize the different procedures, it was an exercise in futility. Even if she could remember all of the moves, she would more often than not sequence the steps in the wrong order. Chris was becoming a Math Avoider. Her psychological response behavior was to turn inward, withdraw, and eventually not even try. Not surprisingly, her negative feelings about math intensified as she grew older.

Robbie did everything quickly—the faster, the better—because he found it less painful. Robbie's reasoning: "It is better to go ahead and do it wrong because you get in less trouble that way." Nothing made much sense in math with all those strange symbols. It didn't seem to matter what he tried, because he was always wrong. He may have gotten the right answer, but he didn't do it the "right" way, so he didn't get any credit for his work. Robbie became another Math Avoider in the making. Both

Robbie and Chris learned to not try anymore. Any curiosity that they may have had about mathematics dwindled away.

Becca had a different experience. When Becca needed her dad's help to complete those homework problems, Becca's dad asked questions rather than telling her how to add the numbers. He helped Becca recognize patterns by circling all of the different problems that had the same sum. Becca noticed several patterns and began to wonder about how this could happen. What was it about these particular numbers that made them have the same "answer" when they were added? Becca's insights developed as she looked deeper into the relationships to "find the ancestors of the patterns,"[2] as third grade Becca described her pattern discoveries.

Robbie's parents and Chris' parents faced the same dilemma that other parents must confront, trying to keep a positive attitude of encouragement with their kids. Mathematics is important for their child's future, at least in the near future for those upcoming standardized tests. How can a parent loosen up on the pressure when the stakes are so high? Whether your child is a Math Avoider, Math Aficionado, or in transition, they can start to think deeply about mathematics by looking for the ancestor patterns in the numbers and behind the formulas. Your child needs to have a safe place to "do math" like no one is watching.

NOTES

1. http://www.brainyquote.com/quotes/quotes/w/waltwhitma146892.html.
2. Whitin, "Becca's Investigation," 81.

Chapter 7

Math Avoiders Are Still Here

If there is a heaven for school subjects, algebra will never go there. It has caused more family rows, more tears, more heartaches, and more sleepless nights than any other school subject. —Anonymous editorial, 1936

Math Avoiders do not wish to experience any more tears, heartaches, or sleepless nights. They have experienced all too many shaming memories associated with learning math; some Math Avoiders have passed the anxiety level and gone straight to phobia. A phobia is defined as a psychological condition relating fear to an experience. For math, the fear is that the shaming experience will happen again. Actually, when the fear reaches phobia level, the fear has escalated into an irrational association with the experience. That Mount Slow-At-Math just got higher and wider with more jagged cliffs.

Any situation that exists when your child experiences learning about numbers can be very powerful and, if negative, can conjure up memories of irrational associations. One self-diagnosed math-phobic Avoider named Anne wrote, "I wasn't born believing that I was unable to perform or even comprehend the simplest of mathematical processes or operations. I received enough messages about my weakness to convince even the dimmest of wits." She continued her story with details about her initial math "failure" because she didn't color the squares green in kindergarten math. She didn't like green. Anne learned to include math on her dislike list.

In the 1980s, Peter Hilton likened "mathophobia" to losing one of the primary senses, as if math could deprive anyone of sight, sound, or touch. Sheila Tobias named the math-associated malady "math anxiety" in her 1978 book. Despite generations of efforts to dispel this traumatic disorder, math anxiety was still widespread enough for the Institute for Neuro-Innovation and Translational Neurosciences at Stanford University to identify the neural correlates of math anxiety in 2012. We are now well into the second decade of the twenty-first century, and the tears, fears, and heartaches that shroud math are still with us.

Whether the heartache is a full-fledged anxiety diagnosis associated with math or is described with a less traumatic-sounding Math Avoider term, the tears still exist.

The Math Avoiders who have these revisiting negative spiraling feelings have a math life existing in a downward "psychospiral." Ever had that feeling of going under? That feeling is what adults have described as they talk about those earlier times when they first started down the math-anxiety path. Just ask any math-phobic person, or Anne.

Listening to stories and reading children's journals confirms that the anxiety isn't about the mathematics; it's about the delivery. It isn't in the message; it's in the message experience. The math phobia comes from confusing the message delivery with the math experience. One solution is to change the delivery of the mathematics so that children can develop a sense of control in their mathematics learning. Before the anxiety has a chance to seed, they can gain a sense of math control by taking back some of the responsibility for their own learning through active involvement through safe and sense-making opportunities.

Removing the following four messages as part of the math experience can go a long way toward keeping the Math Avoider seed from sprouting. The message deliveries to remove from homework math life are stress of success, *premature* precision, shame shackles, and the only-one-right-answer-or-method myth. Successful learning of mathematics does not require any of these inhibitors. Let's take a look at each one and how doses of these inhibitors can have a negative impact when interlaced with the math delivery.

STRESS OF SUCCESS

Stress causes muscle fibers to shorten and the hormone cortisol is released into the body's system. Children are too young for this! Adults don't need it either, but supposedly adults have more control over their stress than children do. Stress can happen when your child mistakenly thinks that they need to be correct *the first time*. Success usually happens *after* mistakes, not before. Just ask Michael Jordan. "I have missed more than 9000 shots in my career. I've lost almost 300 games. I have failed over and over again in my life. And that is why I succeeded."[1]

Over the centuries, many mathematicians have made errors but, like Jordan, turned them into successes. Andrew Wiles' first proof of Fermat's Theorem contained a mistake, yet he turned it around into a famous solution. Alfred Bray Kempe's original proof of the four-color theorem was disproved later but still provided a basis to prove the five-color theorem. Mathematicians have left their marks in history with mathematical mistakes *and* successes. Those who stretch their minds are bound to make some mistakes. However, as Alabama football coach Bear Bryant supposedly cautioned, "just not twice in the same quarter."

PREMATURE PRECISION

Premature precision happens when exactness preempts the overall scope of the mathematical dynamic. Precision and accuracy are important in mathematics, but they only appear as the messy part of the math experimentation is being cleaned up. Some may resent it, be aggravated by it, and even deny it. But you can't make it go away. Precision is part of what makes the end result of mathematics *Mathematics*. There is a time and place for precision such as building a Boeing 747; however, *premature* precision can stifle even the most promising young math thinker. Precision applied too soon can take the fun out of math explorations.

For example, premature precision interrupted mathematical learning for Anne when she didn't want to color the squares green in kindergarten. Anne may have known what a square was, but the square played second fiddle to her dislike of green. But her teacher never knew it was about the color green, not the recognition of the square shape. Another premature precision example happens when any second or third grader is required to place the "1" over the tens column to "record" the regrouping without any experimentation or divergent or lateral thinking ideas about "why" or "reorganization" or simply arranging and rearranging in a different way.

SHAME SHACKLES

There are still too many stories concerning early math experiences in school classrooms when shame is the control tool of choice. These shame stories include descriptions of morbid fear, panic, and absolute wipeout of mental capabilities, along with other descriptions of equally horrifying proportions. All of these feelings are associated with not being able to solve an arithmetic problem—the public shame and guilt of getting a wrong answer.

Shame associated with not being able to work math problems produces more Math Avoiders and not Math Aficionados. Wrong-answer shame is toxic because it sinks into a child's core identity so that they equate their wrong answer with being flawed as a person. The leap from wrong answers to core identity is irrational, and this is what phobias are made of. That loss of core virtue is an isolating experience that paves the way for the irrational belief that they are the only one in the room who still does not understand, and that they are the only one in the galaxy who cannot do math—notice the irrational leap? This memory can be a life sentence.

Usually the misguided objective in employing such shaming behavior is to motivate the child to not make the mistake again, or to study more, or do their homework. Children will remember for sure, but not any of the intended motivators. The memory will be about the shame connected to that math moment and then the math-shame-connection will be shackled together to be avoided at all costs and for as long as humanly possible.

Consider the young child's concept of time/space during their early years in school. The circle graph on the left in Figure 7.1 illustrates an early grade child's perspective on time. When something is happening that is truly fun, that graph turns into something more like the graph on the right when *today* converts to *now*. From this graphing perspective, a child's mental leap from "Today" to "Now" makes sense from their perspective! The irrational leap to "Forever" takes over that large section in the graph during shame. From this perspective, that transition from "I am wrong on this arithmetic problem now" to "I can never do math for forever" can make sense!

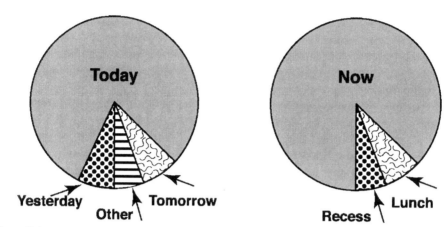

Figure 7.1

ONLY-ONE-RIGHT-ANSWER-OR-METHOD MYTH

For the first eight or so years, the focus in arithmetic is to find "The Answer." This, unfortunately, is a misleading focus. The concentration should be on balance and not on single right answers or on only one "right" method or procedure. George Pólya, the father of problem-solving, proclaimed, "It is better to solve one problem five different ways than to solve five problems one way."[2] Pólya would have appreciated Neil's second grade efforts to figure out different ways and combinations for numbers in equations to balance. Neil played with digit cards on equation mats like the ones in Figure 7.2 and used blocks on the side to test out his number combinations.

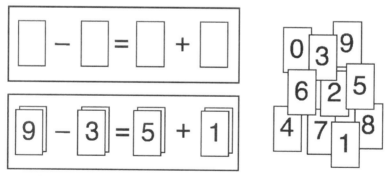

Figure 7.2   Neil's equation mats.

James, a fourth grader, had learned the lattice method for multiplication in the third grade and had become very proficient with it because, to him, everything was organized. Like Robbie, he was subjected to the just-one-way myth when he was required to use the traditional multiplication method despite his continued difficulty with digit placements. After seeing both methods using the same digits in both multiplication methods, James was able to compare the numbers and figure out why the digits were placed for each method. He still preferred the lattice method because it guaranteed his accuracy, but at least he bridged the gap between the methods.

Your child's Math Avoider inner voice may have an aversion to word problems. Instead of asking your child to solve those prefabricated word problems at the end of a section using the method in the section's examples, try to solve these problems differently using Roger von Oech's idea of finding a second right answer, connecting the dots differently, or including a different question or piece of information and then solving the new problem.

The myth of only-one-right-answer is shattered completely when the ambiguity of the algebraic variable appears in a prealgebra or algebra class when several "answers" may make an equation balance. Students have been earnestly seeking the "right answer" for years because they are tested and graded on that one answer in the answer key. There isn't one right method for math problem-solving and there never *has* been only one right method. Some may be more efficient than others, but this is in the eye of the beholder.

SIX THINGS THE MATH AFICIONADO KNOWS THAT THE MATH AVOIDER DOESN'T KNOW

Students, and maybe your child, too, learn quickly and completely how *not* to take control of their own learning when hearing well-meaning encouragement comments such as "just try harder," or "it's easy, just do ..." or "practice makes perfect." All of these phrases effectively deny the emotions that your child might feel relating to any confusion about math. Equally ineffective are the more pejorative comments such as "That's not the way to do it" or "You don't know *that?*" Not taking control and therefore not taking responsibility for their own learning is easier and safer than risking shame, fear, making errors publicly, or being told "no."

No Is Central to K*now*

It takes a "no" and a kink and a wow to make "know"; the seed is "no," the "k" is from the kinks that enable the rethinking, and the "w" is from that audible recognition sound "wow" that seals the deal! The Math Aficionado *expects* to hear a few "no" responses because they realize that the more "no's" that they get sparks their imagination and brings them closer to knowing. August Möbius imagined a one-sided one-edged surface in a two-sided world. Thomas Edison knew ten thousand ways to *not* make a light bulb. Spencer Silver almost did not make the adhesive for Post-it notes because the reports were full of examples that said it couldn't be done.

A helpful counterapproach to a "no" is to use "why" or "when" to ask yourself some questions. Why does it not work now or when would it work? Neil learned about the "when" and the "why" when he placed his digit cards on the equation mats. Anne surmounted her inability to "comprehend the simplest of mathematical processes" by learning later in life to try different approaches when solving math problems. James was able to find out the "why" and "when" for the digit locations when he compared the lattice method with the traditional multiplication process. Celebrate the "no's" with your child to encourage their progress toward the "know's."

Smart Is Good, Regardless of Gender, Race, or Age

"The teacher just called on boys, he didn't think girls could really do math. And also, my friends would get on me for being 'too smart.'"[3] As recently as the nineteenth century, women who became mathematicians were not allowed to study at a university. If they, like Sophie Germain, who was a noted French mathematician during the early part of the nineteenth century, actually published mathematics, then they were required to use a pseudonym. By 1896, culture and mathematical thinking evolved enough for Mary Frances Winston Newson to earn a PhD in mathematics with honors from a European university, the first woman to earn this achievement.

Benjamin Banneker, an eighteenth-century free black man, taught himself mathematics after he left formal school for the tobacco farm where he made his fortune. Elbert Frank Cox, a nineteenth-century mathematician, attended Cornell University and became the first African American in the nation to earn a PhD in mathematics. In 2015, ten-year-old Esther Okade, a British-Nigerian math prodigy, entered Open University, a British distance-learning college.

Your child may or may not be a math prodigy, but they *can* create their own math solution strategies like Bobby, whose fourth grade mind could not keep the division steps in order no matter what mnemonic he followed or how hard he tried. His solution was to make up his own method, a process that made more sense to him. That method looked very similar to an upper-level mathematics process known as interpolation. What's more, Bobby's answers were very, very close to accurate, so he kept interpolating at more and more specific levels until his division answer satisfied his teachers.

Questions May Not Have an Answer Right Away

Math Aficionados are not intimidated by questions. They are reasonably certain that there is an answer, or many answers, somewhere in the near or distant future. The quest is the search for more patterns, more relationships, more algebras, more geometries, and always thinking new thoughts. The math patterns and relationships are already there just for the finding. Your child can also kick-start their curiosity by asking "what if" questions: "What if elephants could fit in this room. How many would fit?" or "What if a single sheet of newspaper was folded in half 50 times? How thick would the folded sheet be?"[4]

Knowledge Isn't Finite

Math Aficionados recognize that they do not know everything about mathematics. This is the real secret. They do not require that they know everything, because if they did the search would end. Also, all mathematicians are not the best at everything that is labeled "mathematics." Some focus on algebra like Srinivasa Ramanujan, some work with other geometries like Nicolai Lobachevski, and some, like Frederich Gauss, delve into number theory. Others, like Benoit Mandelbrot, explore new fractal mathematics and then name these new pattern designs Mandelbrot Sets. All had very healthy imaginations.

The *thinking* involved in mathematics is the important take-away piece of learning mathematics. Math is communicated predominantly in symbols, but not exclusively.

A perusal through Archimedes' drawings, Escher's woodcut art, or any of the current Internet sites illustrating mathematical relationships will provide all the supporting information that you need to recognize the value of thinking and visualization in mathematical thought.

Your child may not end up choosing mathematics as a career, but their career will definitely require a healthy imagination and logical thought, whether it is a part-to-whole logic or a whole-to-part context logic. They will more than likely need to incorporate a healthy dose of both as they maneuver through life events. Even though mathematics may not be part of their career of choice, there is no reason that your child cannot be a Math Aficionado. Not all Math Aficionados are mathematicians, but all mathematicians are Math Aficionados.

Arithmetic Is the Communicator of Mathematics

The age-old quadrivium outline of mathematics[5] illustrated in Figure 7.3 dates back to Plato's *Republic* and shows a kind of family tree for Mathematics. Arithmetic is one of the great-grandchildren of Mathematics, with a Discrete Math grandfather and an Absolute father. Arithmetic includes the collection of number symbols, their compositions, decompositions, and operational combinations—the communication. This diagram can help keep arithmetic in perspective as it relates to the rest of mathematics. It is a reminder that your child's arithmetic is part of a larger scope of mathematical thinking and communicating with numbers and symbols.

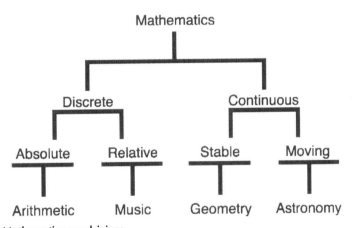

Figure 7.3 Mathematics quadrivium.

Think of mathematics as looking at your child's arithmetic assignments from a helicopter level; there is a larger scope of mathematical thinking where arithmetic serves as the grammar in the math language. Plato's quadrivium shows arithmetic as the "communicator" for music, geometry, and astronomy. The numbers in arithmetic are "freed" from the restrictions of the pictures or objects and can mathematically describe the relationships in other applications. Mathematics is the systematic thinking behind logic, combinatorics, number theory, calculus, and other systems. Some of these systems may be waiting for your child to recognize them.

Mathematics Is Not a Drive Through or Sprint

So, what if you cannot mentally calculate arithmetic calculations faster than a speeding bullet? Mathematics is not a quick pickup at a drive-through window or a speeding-bullet-rate sprint to the corner store. Speed is important when there is a predator afoot or even for a quick dinner but not for productive mathematical thinking. Mathematical thinking takes time—a lot of it and sometimes over a very long period. Over 350 years and many mathematicians' efforts *after* Fermat first suggested a proof in the margin of a math book, Andrew Wiles finally proved the theorem that mathematicians have named Fermat's Last Theorem.

Tests have time limits so timing can sometimes be an important consideration. However, your child isn't necessarily supposed to complete all of the test questions. The tests must include a wide range of mathematics to challenge a wide range of abilities. Also, the mathematics questions on these tests are written to represent problems with solutions developed *after* the longer mathematics thinking time has happened *earlier*. Just doing more problems and learning how to solve specific problems does not help your child *really* prepare for these tests. The preparation is in the time-consuming *mathematics thinking* to solve problems *before* the test.

Good math problems do not always require the same run-of-the-mill solution strategies. Good problems require thinking, strategizing, and rethinking so that on test day the problems do not seem so threatening. One kind of problem to solve *before* the test could be about finding the surface area of a sphere. Von Oech might imagine peeling an orange. Oranges aren't allowed in the test, but your child's imagination is. Figure 7.4 shows an orange peeled and placed on four circles that are center slice cuts of the same orange. With this in their mind's eye, your child can calculate the surface area of a sphere with $4\pi r^2$ or cover those four circles with the orange peel.

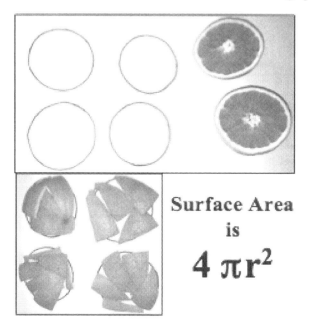

Figure 7.4

KEEP IN MIND

No question is too large, too small, too comprehensive, or too insignificant for good mathematical thinking. Many questions don't have answers just yet. The best questions do not have obvious answers. Curious minds ask the best questions. Sometimes asking one question leads to another and another. More questions lead to more journeys and more journeys lead to more information and the trip continues straight on 'til morning.

NOTES

1. http://www.brainyquote.com/quotes/quotes/m/michaeljor127660.html.
2. http://www.azquotes.com/quote/739949.
3. Hersh, *Loving + Hating Math*, 304.
4. Answer: Newspaper folds reach the sun: http://sploid.gizmodo.com/if-you-fold-a-paper-in-half-103-times-it-will-be-as-thi-1607632639.
5. Turnbull, *The Great Mathematicians*, 11.

Chapter 8

Math Aficionados at Work

Mathematics [is] infinitely complex and magical world; exploring it is an addiction from which [we] hope never to be cured.[1] —Philip Davis and Reuben Hersh

Math Aficionados have not forgotten how to play even though they may have grown up chronologically. They play with mathematical relationships while thinking mathematically and they are vigilant about discovering different patterns and new relationships. Math Aficionados are confident that these elements are there *somewhere*, even if they do not see them right away. While they search, they imagine unusual connections as they meander through a "Math Wonderland" of curious and sometimes nonconforming and unusual ideas.

Math Aficionados compare, sort, classify, visualize, sketch, and analyze in their search to find new patterns and relationships. They even ask questions that they cannot answer. They strategically guess (conjecture in math-speak), make predictions, fix any errors in their guesses, and continue to conjecture while getting closer and closer to finding at least one solution. This persistence requires curiosity, perseverance, and confidence. Math Aficionados work toward finding a way to generalize their patterns and then prove them, leaving no ambiguous stones unturned. This proof effort can take hours, days, weeks, or years, and oftentimes centuries.

A few Math Aficionados have described this seeking as "math spelunking"; others have proclaimed it a voyage of discovery. Math Aficionados find mathematics "curiouser and curiouser" while seeking solutions. Lewis Carroll, a mathematician and clearly a Math Aficionado, whose real name was Charles Dodgson, gave voice to his mathematical thinking through his 1865 novel *Alice's Adventures in Wonderland*, leaving the reader to wonder if this adventure could be his idea of how mathematicians played with mathematics. Does a Math Aficionado look for solutions, find them, and then smile like the satisfied Cheshire Cat?

SPELUNKING FOR PATTERNS

Geometry and other space and picture problems offer good opportunities for encouraging your visual-spatial child to play with math like the Math Aficionados. A typical geometry picture in Figure 8.1 offers several patterns for the math spelunker. All of the shapes are regular—meaning all sides have equal measures and all the angles are equal to each other. A math spelunker might see triangles inside each of the shapes and be curious about a possible relationship between the number of sides and the number of triangles. The math spelunker in your child might also be curious about the missing triangle and the nonagon.

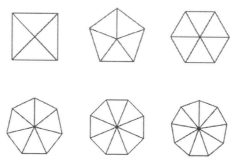

Figure 8.1

The conjecture by a Math Aficionado spelunker about the missing nonagon (nine-sided shape) and triangle might be about whether these missing polygons could also have the same triangle arrangements like the polygons shown in Figure 8.2. A math spelunker might also wonder if the total angle measures in *all* of the triangles in the polygon had anything to do with the 360° in a circle. If that math spelunker knew about protractors, then they might measure the angles *around the perimeter corner edges* and keep a record of *all* of the angles and degrees shown in Figure 8.2 while getting a better idea about the whole concept picture.

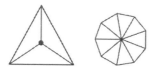

Regular Polygon Shapes								
	△	⊠	⬠	⬡	⬡	⯃	⯃	⯃
Number of inner triangles	3	4	5	6	7	8	9	10
Total degrees in the polygon	540°	720°	900°	1080°	1260°	1440°	1620°	1800°
Total of angle degrees around the perimeter	180°	360°	540°	720°	900°	1080°	1260°	1440°

Figure 8.2

Pretty soon that Cheshire Cat smile begins to show on the Math Aficionado's face because, like Claire, they start recognizing more patterns and start conjecturing about more relationships. Claire, a high-school Algebra I student, had many questions to ask and even more patterns to find. Her curiosity about the polygons in Figure 8.1 inspired her to conjecture about increases in the number of degrees. By collecting data, she was able to identify an algebra pattern that she eventually converted into an equation. Claire decided that the nonagon would have at least 200 fewer degrees than the decagon. Eventually, she decided on 180° as the magic number.

Claire said that 1260° was the total number of degrees for the missing nonagon and explained it by saying, "Each time the number of sides grows, I am squeezing in another triangle and triangles have 180°." Using the linear equation template from her Algebra I class ($y = mx + b$), Claire wrote $y = 180x$ ("y" equals the total number of degrees and "x" equals the number of sides). No need for the "b" in the format, so at this stage the "b" would equal zero. Claire kept her data in a table shown in Figure 8.3 to show how she imagined the increase of 180° as the number of triangles kept increasing.

Claire's Table of collected data					
Number of sides	3	4	5	...	x
Number of triangles	3	4	5	...	x
Total number of degrees (y)	540	720	900	...	180 x

Figure 8.3   Claire's work.

Her next idea was to figure out how many degrees were in *each* angle around the rim of the polygon. After thinking a bit, Claire noticed that her "Total degrees in the polygon" data in her table included *all* of the degrees in *all* of the triangles, not just the angles on the outer perimeter rim so she subtracted the 360° that would be in the circle made by all of those center angles at the top of the triangles. She wrote the equation $180x - 360$ in order to get rid of those center angles. Now she had a way to calculate the total number of degrees in *all* of those angles around the rim of the polygon.

Claire realized that the total of all of the base angles of the triangles also matched the total number of degrees in the angles on the outer rim of the polygon so, after pondering a bit more, she decided to divide by the number of sides. Now she knew the number of degrees in just *one* of the angles of the polygon. She devised her own algebra formula using her linear equation thinking and applied it to geometry patterns!

Claire "squeezed in" a new triangle each time the number of sides increased, while another student, a fourth grader named Nick, saw these same shapes and guessed that the triangles were fractional parts of the shapes. In Nick's mind, more cuts would make smaller pieces. Both students persisted and eventually generated their idea of a "proof" to support their assertions. Claire made a table and conjectured from the numbers; Nick chose a different shape, a rectangle, because it would be easier to cut. He used several same-sized rectangles, as shown in Figure 8.4, and cut each rectangle into more and more equal-sized, smaller pieces.

Figure 8.4   Nick's fraction cuts.

Nick's description was expressed in his own words with "First I folded the rectangle in half and cut it. Next I folded another rectangle in half and half again to make four pieces to cut out. The next fold was the same as the last and then I folded it again in half. The last fold gave me 16 pieces. Each time I cut I got more pieces than before, but the pieces were getting smaller every time." A Math Aficionado might express this with the phrase "the greater the denominator, the smaller the fractional piece."

PREDICTABLE CHANGES CREATE PATTERNS

Math Aficionados are like the mice Sniff and Scurry in the book *Who Moved My Cheese?* Math Aficionados are not bothered by change. In fact, they like change, the predictable kind, and are willing to sniff out predictable kinds of patterns. Because they are willing to visualize and think differently, Math Aficionados can recognize new patterns in these predictable changes and identify more entries that fit into those patterns by writing different equations. These equations can eventually become functions and are now part of a larger Bigger Idea known as a mathematical system.

One example of a change that happens in math is when numbers are allowed to increase and decrease to enlarge or shrink a design. The square design in Figure 8.5 shows how the "x" on the left large square changes. Instead of an "x" for the second shape, the number "3" replaces the "x," so $x = 3$. This repeats all the way to $x = 1/2$ as the overall square gets smaller. In general, as the x value changes, the overall square design changes. As the shaded square gets smaller, the edges of the overall square also change accordingly from $(x + 1)(x + 1)$ to $(3 + 1)(3 + 1)$ to $(2 + 1)(2 + 1)$ to $(1 + 1)$ $(1 + 1)$ and then $((1/2) + 1)((1/2) + 1)$. Sniff, Scurry, and Math Aficionados can deal with changes.

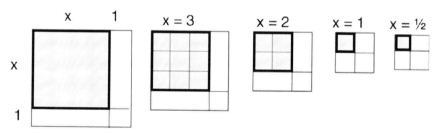

Figure 8.5   How the "x" can shrink.

Your child might be one of those students who has a peculiar magnet that attracts only positive whole numbers to substitute into any algebraic expression. When faced with using 0.5 or one-half as an option for the "*x*" value, that "*x*" needs to shrink smaller than one unit, a change in unit perspective. When Robin Williams' character in the 1989 movie *Dead Poets Society* told his students to stand on their desks, he was suggesting that they see life from a different perspective. Everything can seem to shrink from atop a chair, so if your child imagines standing on a chair, then they can imagine looking down in order to "see" the shrinking effect on "*x*."

What an interesting way to look at change! The math version of a different perspective to increase or decrease can happen when your child stands on the chair to look down or lies on the floor to look up. Their normal view changes, like when the "*x*" reduces from $x = 1$ to $x = 1/2$ or when "*x*" is assigned a large number, larger than three, ten, or any large number. Because the predictable kind of change is one of the Big Ideas in mathematics, relationships will always be tested with larger numbers, smaller numbers, and all kinds of numbers in between.

The design from Figure 8.5 enlarges to a much bigger square when $x = 10$ shown in Figure 8.6 and takes on a more familiar arithmetic relationship that may remind you of the third grade two-digit multiplication problem that looks like 11×11. The 11×11 design is the same as the algebra version from Figure 8.5 when looking "up" from $x = 3$ to $x = 10$ in the design. Your child might have observed by now that both the overall design of the algebra relationship and the overall multiplication problem represent square shapes.

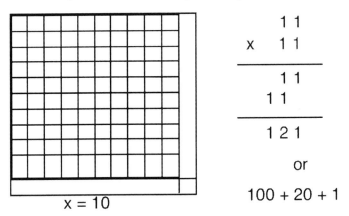

Figure 8.6

DOUBLING SIDES—DOUBLING AREAS? NOT SO FAST

What is so special about similar shapes and the effect on their related measurements? It is about predictability. There is a predictable relationship between changing sides on similar shapes and the areas and volumes of these same shapes. It isn't just change; it is about *how* the changes happen and the *predictable rate* of change. With all of the changes that your child can control with sides and angles of triangles and quadrilaterals and even polygons, they may expect that the *same* kind of change will happen with relationships involving comparing perimeters, areas, and volumes between two similar shapes. Time to investigate and test this expectation.

Changing the length of all of the sides of a shape by the same multiple will make the two shapes similar, but how will changing the side change the area? As an example, if all of the sides of a shape are doubled, does the area of that shape double? To answer this question, your child can draw polygons, double the side lengths, and keep a record. Math Aficionados, and your child too, can test the easy ones first, so start with a small equilateral triangle like the one in Figure 8.7. Double all sides of that triangle to make the larger triangle. Then place the original small triangle inside the doubled-length side larger triangle.

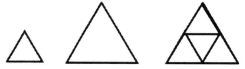

Figure 8.7

Imagination, visual-spatial eyes-that-see, some old-fashioned tracing paper, and geometric rotations are good ingredients for exploring and investigating. Imagine the smaller triangle inside the larger doubled-length side triangle and then look for some pattern relationship clues. How many of the small triangles fit without overlaps inside the larger triangle? Would your child have guessed that the area of the larger triangle is actually four times the area of the smaller triangle?

Let's examine other triangles that are not equilateral to see what happens. The isosceles triangle and the scalene triangle in Figure 8.8 show the side lengths that are doubled for each kind of triangle, keeping the shapes similar. The original small triangle is then placed inside the larger one to see how many times the smaller triangle will fit into the larger one without overlaps, but rotations are allowed. The center small triangle in both isosceles and scalene triangles is rotated to fit inside the larger doubled-length sided triangle. In both cases, the larger triangles' areas are made from four of the smaller similar triangles.

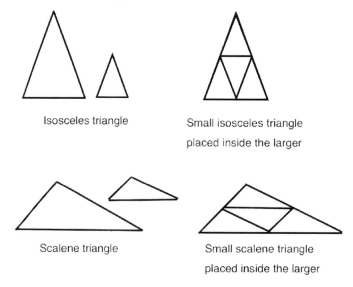

Isosceles triangle

Small isosceles triangle
placed inside the larger

Scalene triangle

Small scalene triangle
placed inside the larger

Figure 8.8

The initial triangle examples will make a curious young Math Aficionado start to wonder about other polygons and how doubling the sides changes those areas.

Continue to gradually increase the difficulty from triangles to multisided polygons, testing at each stage. Some mistakes are expected, even welcomed, so they might as well start with some simple shapes, like rectangles and parallelograms, to improve their chances for success. In Figure 8.9, the rectangles and parallelograms show how doubling the sides of a rectangle and parallelogram allows enough space for four of the small shapes to fit inside the larger doubled-length side shape.

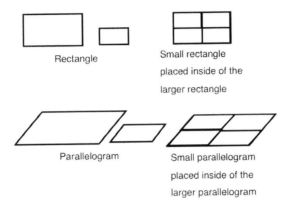

Rectangle   Small rectangle
placed inside of the
larger rectangle

Parallelogram   Small parallelogram
placed inside of the
larger parallelogram

Figure 8.9

The regular pentagon and isosceles trapezoid do not easily fit inside their doubled-side length larger similar shape. If the small shape is placed into the larger shape in the same manner as the triangle and parallelogram, then overlaps happen. The small trapezoids do not fill the space in the large trapezoid without overlaps and the small pentagons do not fit nicely without overlaps either. However, Figure 8.10 shows how both the trapezoid and the pentagon were decomposed into triangles. When the number of triangles in the small shape is compared with the number of triangles in the doubled-length side shape, then the areas can be compared.

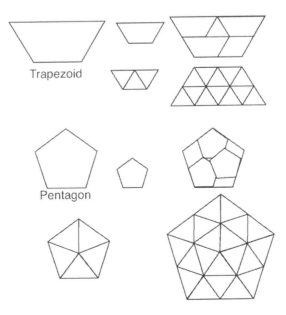

Trapezoid

Pentagon

Figure 8.10

Decomposing both the isosceles trapezoid and the regular pentagon into congruent triangles allows the rearrangement necessary to show how doubling a side affects the area. Three equilateral triangles will fill the small isosceles trapezoid. Use those triangles, and more, to fill the doubled-side trapezoid and then count the triangles. The small pentagon decomposes into five small isosceles triangles (not equilateral) and then lots of those triangles can be used to fill the inside of the larger pentagon, rearrangements and rotations allowed. Count the triangles in the area of the large pentagon. Compare the areas in both sizes for both trapezoid and pentagon.

The regular hexagon has the same overlapping difficulty that the pentagon and the trapezoid have. Triangles come to the rescue! (Have you recognized the same kinds of triangles from the Figure 8.2 design? There's a connection.) The regular hexagon shape is one of the Pattern Blocks, so your child can compare the number of triangles in the small hexagon with the larger hexagon as shown in Figure 8.11. Decomposing the hexagon into six equilateral (and also isosceles) triangles and using these same-sized triangles to cover the doubled-length sided hexagon shows that it takes 24 triangles to cover the larger hexagon. Yes, it's four times more.

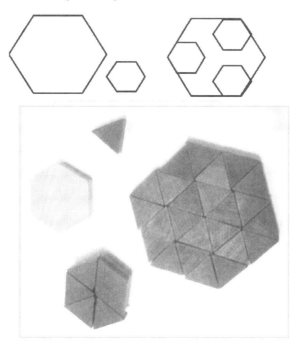

Figure 8.11

Don't stop now if your child's imagination is in full gear. Try the regular octagon. Try the regular nonagon and the decagon. Draw the lines of symmetry or trace and fold the shapes to locate the center of each regular polygon. After locating the center, draw line segments from the center to each vertex (corner). Isosceles triangles in Figure 8.12 fit inside a regular octagon, regular nonagon, and regular decagon, different triangles for each polygon. Try any of the other regular polygons. Try tripling the sides of the polygons. Your child can use Pattern Blocks, Parquetry Blocks, or tracing paper to help visualize the shape decompositions.

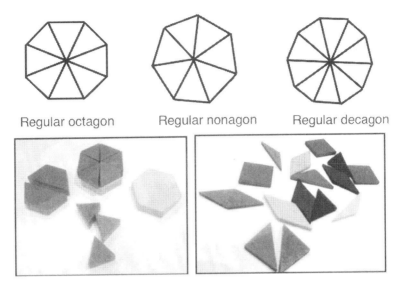

Regular octagon   Regular nonagon   Regular decagon

Figure 8.12

Your child may have already recognized the pattern. The area of a doubled-length sided shape is always four times the area of its smaller similar shape. The area of a tripled-length sided shape is always nine times the area of the smaller shape. Math Aficionados, and now your child, too, have completed the tables in Figure 8.13 and figured out the pattern prediction between doubling and tripling side lengths of similar shapes and their related areas. It always helps to keep track of trial data in a table when looking for patterns and relationships. What about quadrupling sides? What about multiplying side lengths by five? More data for the table!

Areas are a two-dimensional measurement. What do you think would happen with one-dimensional lengths with perimeters in the same doubled-length sided and tripled-length sided shapes? Start with easy examples. Conjecture, confirm your conjecture, adjust your conjecture if necessary, and make a table of the data you collect. Later in algebra your child will see the equations for square areas as $y = x^2$, so when the side (x) is doubled, then the area (y) will be $y = (2x)^2$ and when tripled $y = (3x)^2$. Now add the sides for a perimeter. How do you think the perimeters in Figure 8.13 would be shown in algebra?[2]

Area						
Shape	△	▭	▽	▱	⬠	⬡
Sides x 2	x 4	x 4	x 4	x 4	x 4	x 4
Sides x 3	x 9	x 9	x 9	x 9	x 9	x 9

Figure 8.13

Perimeter						
Shape	△	▭	▽	▱	⬠	⬡
Sides x 2	x 2	x 2	x 2	x 2	x 2	x 2
Sides x 3	x 3	x 3	x 3	x 3	x 3	x 3

Figure 8.13 *Continued*

VOLUMES FOLLOW SUIT

The perimeters and the areas have predictable patterns. Do volumes? Finding volumes requires a jaunt into three-dimensional shapes. Try doubling all three of the dimensional sides of the first small "shoebox" prism—double the width, double the length, and double the height. Conjecture *first* about the number of shoeboxes in Figure 8.14 that would fit into the larger doubled-length side shoeboxes and *then* count them. Start your testing with a rectangular "shoebox" prism since it is one of the easier examples to investigate.

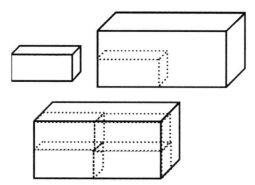

Figure 8.14

As the examples increase in difficulty, the more important it is to keep a record. After trying several doubled-length sided polyhedra, try some tripled-length sided examples. Test the doubled-length sided relationship for cubes. Count the small cubes that fit inside the doubled-length sided cube. There should be four cubes on the bottom layer with four more on top for the doubled-length sided cube for a total of eight cubes. For a tripled-length side cube, also shown in Figure 8.15, there should be nine cubes on the bottom layer, nine cubes in the middle layer, and another nine cubes on the top layer.

Stacking one-inch cube blocks shows how doubling and tripling the sides of cubes make larger, similar-shaped cubes. Nothing is as clear to young learners, indeed all visual-spatial learners, as the actual experience of stacking blocks. For those inclined to do the algebraic calculations, that works quite well, too. The algebra equation for the single-cube volume will look like $V = x^3$ and $V = (2x)^3$ for the volume in the doubled-length side and $V = (3x)^3$ for tripled-length sides. Let the "x" be the value for the first side length and let "V" be the volume.

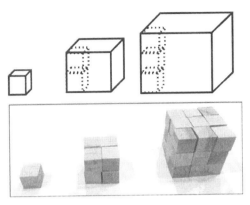

Figure 8.15

Feeling adventurous? How about the cylinder? Do you suppose the volume relationship will also apply to cylinders like the ones shown in Figure 8.16? Do the cylinders stack nicely? Would a Math Aficionado need to use some arithmetic or maybe even algebra to actually calculate the volumes and compare the amounts? Don't forget to use the pi ratio with the radius to calculate the areas of the bottom of the cylinders. Keep a record of the areas of the base as the wall heights increase from single to double to triple heights.

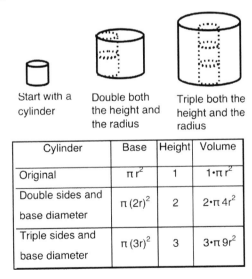

Cylinder	Base	Height	Volume
Original	πr^2	1	$1 \cdot \pi r^2$
Double sides and base diameter	$\pi (2r)^2$	2	$2 \cdot \pi 4r^2$
Triple sides and base diameter	$\pi (3r)^2$	3	$3 \cdot \pi 9r^2$

Figure 8.16

All of the volumes from the different solids assembled into one table in Figure 8.17 make it easier to recognize a pattern. The volumes for all of the solids have a predictable increase. Like the cube in Figure 8.15 and the cylinder in Figure 8.16, when the side lengths double for polyhedra, the volume is eight times more, and when the side lengths are tripled, the volume is 27 times more.

Volume			
Shape			 (Diameter)
Sides x 2	x 8	x 8	x 8
Sides x 3	x 27	x 27	x 27

Figure 8.17

Polydrons, Magformers, and those kindergarten Froebel blocks will give your curious and budding Math Aficionado child some valuable exploration in visual and tactile math activities. The blocks can be used across all grade levels, depending on the mathematical application. If Polydrons and Magformers are not in your pantry, then tracing paper, cardboard empty boxes, and cutouts of construction paper can work just as well. The idea is to get your child involved in making the mathematics. If your child physically moves the items to show different relationships, then their vision of mathematics encourages more curiosity and more satisfaction and improves their flexible thinking.

KEEP IN MIND

When your child learns that they can actually build these shapes to see the patterns, their math life changes significantly. The next stage is to develop flexibility and control around the composing (building up) and decomposing (taking apart) of both numbers and shapes. Your child will start to realize that this assembly and disassembly actually works with both numbers and shapes. They will begin to understand *how* they *can* have control over their math. Compositions, decompositions, and rearrangement can be a math world–enlarging event.

NOTES

1. Davis, *The Mathematical Experience*, 1.
2. Answer: If "x" is the perimeter of the small shape, then $2x$ is the perimeter of the doubled-length larger shape. So, "y" can now represent the perimeter of the larger shape: $y = 2x$.

Chapter 9

Insight Is an Inside Job

We do not know in advance who will discover fundamental insights.[1]
—Carl Sagan

Your child just might be the next one to discover one of those insights in math. Gaining insight comes from within; you cannot give it to your child but you *can* provide some insight-provoking experiences so that your child can develop their own insightful thinking in mathematics. Insight is all about connecting concepts and probing deeper when *thinking* about mathematical relationships. Your child recognizes this insightful experience with that aha moment when ideas fall into place. The experience of recognizing connections among several ideas is individualized, personal, and unique to each person.

Insight can be nurtured by asking questions. Just as the Math Aficionado asks questions to promote thinking, you and your child can, too. The best questions can make your child think more deeply or differently that could lead to some "out of the box" ideas. One of Edward de Bono's strategies to instigate "lateral thinking" is to not use words at all but to instead use diagrams and visuals that represent the problems *that are upside down*. One of Roger von Oech's "soft thinking" tools toward thinking differently is to describe a problem with a metaphor, such as "a math jigsaw solution to a problem."

HANDS-ON INSIGHT

Dictionaries will classify "insight" as a noun and describe it as an ability to gain a deeper intuitive understanding of some situation or thing. A math example that comes to mind is when Greg, a strongly motivated high-school student, was trying desperately to understand what a square root had to do with a square despite many verbal explanations and even a few pictures. He eventually used a pair of scissors and a grid sheet to cut out a square that had 25 units. By the time he was cutting out the third side, he put down both the scissors and grid paper with the audible, satisfied, and delightful-to-hear acclamation, "I get it!"

In the process of cutting out that square from grid paper, Greg's mind started putting ideas together. Greg gained insight through his hands; he recognized the relationship between squares and square roots, between squares and sides, and between perimeter and area. Greg and Paul, another high-school student, had a lot in common in that they both gained that deeper understanding through their hands.

Paul, who was adept at woodworking, gained some math insight through his hands. Paul was trying to understand how a cone cut could help "see" conic section equations (the format when set equal to 1). Paul sliced a wooden cone model shown in Figure 9.1 after he turned it on the lathe in woodworking shop. The photos show how he cut the sections of the cones. The circle came from a horizontal cut on one cone (adding same denominator), the ellipse had a slant cut on one cone (adding different denominators), the hyperbola outline had a vertical cut across both cones (more different denominators and subtracted), and the parabola had one careful slant cut.

Figure 9.1   Paul's cones.

Math insights are not reserved for older students. Insights can happen with your child at any age when several associations and connections come together in their thinking. A second grader delightfully declared, "I know why you are teaching me with these shape blocks. This is just like those base ten blocks." She had connected the idea of organizing the numbers in place value and organizing and sorting shapes. A sixth grader asked, "Is this [separating and comparing] the same as Patch [a fraction game]?" He had internalized the relationship between two topics, division and fractions. Now, the topics made sense to each child.

A fifth grader named Jean was learning about circles, and none of the information stayed in memory long enough to connect to anything else. She seemed to know and understand one day and the following day the same information was mixed up and confused. Like Greg and Paul, she was more successful when she "saw" through her hands. She used a round coffee filter and folded it so that one side of the circle matched the other (symmetry). Then she folded it again. At this point, the conversation became interesting. Jean started asking about the folds and sections shown in Figure 9.2, and then new Bigger Idea questions started to pour out of her mind.

Figure 9.2   Jean's coffee filters.

Jean was curious about how closely this coffee filter folding resembled those fraction pictures she had learned earlier and the clock numbers from a few years back.

She was also curious, like Nick, about how many different folds she could make to have different sizes of sections. The insight connections started to take on new and different approaches. Just by listening to her own questions and observations, Jean created her own mental pictures of some mathematical relationships. Now that the mental picture images were in her head, the naming of the folds, the sections, and all those other items were easy for her to remember.

MATH ABSTRACTIONS TOO SOON

Math problems are often presented as written words and a drawing on two-dimensional paper, even though the math problem may be about relationships in a three-dimensional setting. For very young children, the picture is already one level into abstraction and the words may represent yet another level of abstraction. If the initial presentation is already abstract, then they have little chance of making sense of the math relationships. Jean Piaget, Friedrich Froebel, and pre-kindergarten teachers know that, to an early learning child, a two-dimensional drawing bears little resemblance to a three-dimensional object because spatial perception isn't well developed.

If math is only presented at the abstraction level in two dimensions as a pencil-and-paper math, then young children grow up without making the dimensional connection of mathematics to reality. The math is always abstract to them. The visual-spatial or visual-mechanical child will always be handicapped with mathematics unless they have an opportunity to associate the math connection to relationships between real three-dimensional objects.

For visual-spatial learners, connections and understandings usually follow a spatial recognition of relationships among objects translated through diagrams, comparisons, or intuitive thinking. Jean could draw on her coffee filters to make those connections for herself, Greg could cut out the square, and Paul could recognize how the slices affected the equations. Cultivating insights with your child has a longer-term benefit for maintaining memory. Gardner tells us that memory is intelligence specific so it seems reasonable to let your child's mind to do most of the intelligence work. Your child will remember more and for a longer period of time.

A group of researchers studying the insight experience found "evidence that the right hemisphere plays a unique role in insight."[2] All human brains have a right hemisphere so it would follow that all of us *can have* insights given the appropriate experiences. With these appropriate experiences, insights in mathematics are equal opportunity events. Let's return to Greg's insight with squares and square roots by delving further into some of the many ways that a square is used in mathematical relationships.

THE SQUARES HAVE IT

Greg could see the square as a shape first and then made some connections to other relationships with squares. Your child was likely introduced to the square shape in pre-kindergarten and continued to use it just as a shape before later learning that numbers can be arranged into a square shape. These square numbers started appearing very early in place value with 100 using 10 × 10 units. A year or so later, that square had an area that was calculated by multiplying the two lengths of its adjacent sides.

The square is a regular quadrilateral with more congruent parts than any of the other quadrilaterals. Because of its regularities and congruencies, the calculations with squares show up in quite a few mathematical relationships and formulas. Squares are used from generating perfect square numbers to calculations in statistics and from the Pythagorean Theorem areas to binomial squared notations in algebra. Let's explore a few of these square calculations as they appear in different topics and in different levels of math concepts.

At some point in math, your child will learn about numbers that are called perfect squares, the numbers that are calculated with whole numbers and also represent square areas. Those perfect square numbers are located on the diagonal of the multiplication table. Then there are square figurate numbers, when a number of items can be arranged into a square shape. Along come the gnomons for squares in Figure 9.3 when the odd numbers that are added to each preceding square arrangement number to make a new square number. Let the patterns continue!

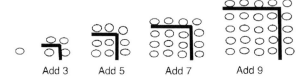

| Add 3 | Add 5 | Add 7 | Add 9 |

Figure 9.3

The Pythagoreans probably used square shapes to show how the sides of a right triangle are related. They calculated areas that matched to the triangle sides and added the two smaller areas to get the largest area like the ones shown in Figure 9.4. They wrote it with symbols using $a^2 + b^2 = c^2$ and proved that this relationship *only* applied to the sides of right triangles. The Pythagoreans might have split up the medium-sized square into triangles. Next, they could have played around with combining and rearranging the pieces in the "b^2" and "a^2" squares to see if the new square would match the largest "c^2" square. It did.

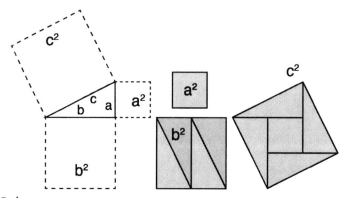

Figure 9.4   Pythagorean rearrangement.

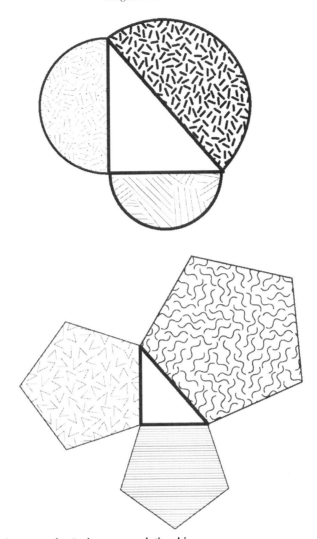

Figure 9.4a Other areas for Pythagorean relationship.

The Pythagoreans were not the first to use this idea, but they did secure the naming rights to this relationship because they were the first to "prove" the relationship. This adding-the-areas-of-sides relationship also works when the medium-sized square and the small square have the same area, making the triangle an isosceles right triangle. In fact, areas of any similar shapes (these are measured in square units) constructed from the sides of a right triangle, like the ones in Figure 9.4a, will also have this $a^2 + b^2 = c^2$ relationship of areas, but the square is probably easier to recognize. Maybe Bill was right; it isn't easy being a square.

Are you feeling adventurous? How flexible is your child (or you) with your spatial sense? Your child can take this same Pythagorean arrangement with squares, take them apart (decompose them) to make triangles, and rearrange those pieces into another larger arrangement. To accomplish this, the c^2 square shape is decomposed and rearranged to create the sides of a much larger square shown on the right-hand side in Figure 9.5 that also includes the original b^2 square. The algebra-speak for this new square is a quadratic binomial squared, or, in symbol form, $(a + b)^2$. This binomial square relationship is used as early as fourth grade in multiplying numbers.

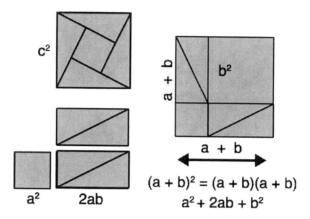

Figure 9.5

The square is expressed within an algebra equation with $y = x^2$ shown on one of the cards in the *Algebra Game*[3] and matched with its related graph card and coordinate point table shown in Figure 9.6. That very small "2" exponent located in the upper right position of "x" is read as "x squared" because the "2" means that the x could be a side of a virtual square. The square has migrated across grade levels and math topics from a square shape to a square number, and now as part of a larger algebraic relationship that includes connections to graphs, coordinate pairs, and algebraic equations. Algebraic equations with squares as relationships are also used in statistics.

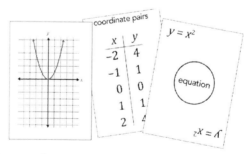

Figure 9.6   *Algebra Game* cards.

STATISTICS AND SQUARES

In a statistics class, an area calculated under a graph curve represents the variance of the data. The picture in Figure 9.7 shows an imaginary normal graph curve with an imaginary variance square area. As one very astute high-school student quietly reminded me, a square area doesn't *have* to be a square; it is a number. So, because the variance area *can* be rearranged into a square area, the edge of that square would represent the square root and the square root shows the location of the first standard deviation (a way to figure out the spread of data) from the mean. Squares and square areas and square roots are useful, so they keep coming back.

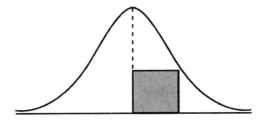

Figure 9.7 Normal curve.

A good question for a Math Aficionado to ask is "What is it about a square that makes it so useful for expressing or calculating math relationships?" Like the mathematician, you do not have to know the answer in order to ask the question. Also like the mathematician, the questioning encourages your child to compare properties of squares with other quadrilaterals, triangles, and polygons and the related calculations associated with the polygons to investigate why it is so different. Let the spelunking begin!

WHAT'S IN A SQUARE ROOT?

Like most middle-school students, the Pythagoreans certainly preferred the perfect squares; however, during their searches for new relationships with numbers and shapes, the Pythagoreans kept looking and eventually identified the existence of squares that turned out not to be perfect squares. To their dismay, and to middle schoolers too, those squares had sides that were not whole numbers. These new kinds of numbers still measured the adjacent sides of a square, but the Pythagoreans did not know what middle schoolers now know—that with a little help from their calculators, the side calculates to a decimal version of an irrational number.

The Pythagoreans did not have floor tiles like the ones bought these days at a home supply store, but they did have floor coverings. Maybe their idea of squares came from a floor design and the side of that square had to be something that they could calculate. A twenty-first-century version of a Pythagorean floor tile design is a one-foot square tile, and the side of that twenty-first-century floor tile is the length of a one-foot ruler. Both square tile and ruler in Figure 9.8 are used here to represent measurements, one for area and one for length. The square root can be thought of as the bridge between the area of the square and the side measure of that square.

Figure 9.8   Square tile and square root ruler.

The side of the floor tile matches the length of the ruler so the length of the ruler can represent the square root, another visual way to get hands-on and heads-around the concept. So, the square root of a number (shown as a square foot area) is a number that is a side length for that area number. This idea represents a change from a two-dimensional area to a one-dimensional length, the inverse of multiplying two adjacent side lengths (one-dimension) to get a two-dimensional area. This dimension change makes Greg's difficulty more understandable.

Another example for square roots could be Greg's smaller floor tile with 25 square inches with the side measure of five inches. The square root of 25 square units is 5 length units. As long as the square areas have whole-number ruler length sides, the square is called a perfect square. But if the tile area is 24 square inches, the ruler will have a length of 4.8989794 … and continues without a pattern. This decimal number will not have repeating pattern nor does it have a stopping place, so 24 is not a perfect square number, making $\sqrt{24}$ an irrational number. Not ending and not having a pattern sound like two good reasons to call that number irrational.

As squares increase in area, so do their side measures. Todd, a fifth grade student, used the Pythagorean relationship to generate a spiral from lengths of "growing" right triangles shown in Figure 9.9. Todd used square roots to calculate each new hypotenuse (longest side) of each larger right triangle. Different calculations make different spirals. A high-school student created the spiral garden and a middle-school student used his computer programming knowledge to generate his color spiral. Spirals can be generated with calculations as long as there is a predictable change in the mix.

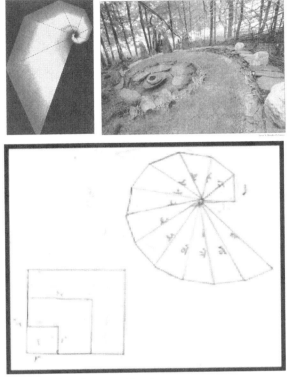

Figure 9.9   *Source*: Garden photo by Jason Henske.

SQUARES TO CUBES AND …

If your child imagines a square that is stackable (has depth), then that square could stack to make a cube and that same square would also be one side of the surface area of that same cube. A cube is one of the Platonic solids, and these solids have very specific relationships of sides and angles. That square surface side of the cube isn't the only regular shape that can be part of the surface area of a Platonic solid, but it *is* the only one that "stacks" to make up the volume of its related polyhedra.

Figure 9.10   Platonic solids.

It is time for another question. "If a square is the surface side of a cube shown in Figure 9.10 and also could be imagined to 'stack' to make a cube, why doesn't the regular triangle that is part of the surface side of another Platonic tetrahedron 'stack' to make the tetrahedron or icosahedron from the Platonic solids group?" The same question can apply to the other Platonic solids: "Why doesn't the regular pentagon that is part of the surface area of a Platonic solid dodecahedron stack to make a dodecahedron?" Is it time for some more math spelunking?

To start thinking about these questions, your child needs to investigate what makes a Platonic solid so different. Younger Math Aficionado spelunkers can just build these solids and older Math Aficionados will likely analyze the five Platonic solids. These questions will not be on the test nor are they likely to appear in your child's homework, but they are worth asking to generate some insights.

KEEP IN MIND

Math insights are made up of part learning new information, part connecting the pieces, and part intuition. Insight is about getting inside and behind the formulas, learning about and appreciating math relationships. Math insights very often lead to thinking beyond the obvious in order to find the "ancestors" of the numbers. Freedom to explore and experiment is the playground for math insights, and your child will likely enjoy the play if they have "permission" to move math shapes and math concepts in different arrangements in order to see them from different perspectives.

NOTES

1. https://gist.github.com/titipata/42e78ac13a5aa4e94fb7.
2. Bowden, *Psychonomic Bulletin*, 730.
3. Draper, *Algebra Game Quadratic Equations*, deck a.

Part IV

CONNECTIONS

Photography images space.
Dance with tempo fills space.
Sports go through space.
Architecture embraces and encases space.

All of these are artistic configurations within space and all use mathematics to express their respective art forms. Each has a mathematical story to tell about the beauty of form, efficiency, endurance, and heart. Your child is likely to be interested in at least one of them. This section introduces some possible responses to offer when that question heard around every dining room homework table is asked, "When will I use this?"

The three chapters in the Connections section describe how mathematics is involved in each art form for seeing, moving, and building. The two-dimensional visual arts of drawing, painting, printmaking, drafting, design, and photography have similar aspects so chapter 10 addresses a photography story that represents elements shared in these art forms. The photography chapter topics include balance, symmetry of form, and proportions in a vanishing point, all mathematical relationships as well.

The actions involved in sports, including dance, require efficient use of body mechanics for personal best records. Those personal bests are measured with mathematics, not only for speed and accuracy but also for form and facility. Chapter 11 describes the choreography of dance, including a selection of tempo ratios, as it relates to a selection of math activities followed by some short descriptions of competitive sports "choreography" and imaginative field designs that play with ratios.

Chapter 12 is dedicated to architecture as a visual art form of building and the building details involved in the embracing and encompassing of space. Architecture is the visual design and the construction contractor turns this visual design into reality. Both the architect and the contractor must be able to use the language of mathematics in order to bridge the gap between the design of any building and its physical existence.

Where's the math? Anytime your child takes an especially pleasing photo, sinks a basketball into the net, or pockets a numbered ball in a billiards game, mathematics is happening. Anytime you count and compare totals of scores or calculate a batting average, you make numerical comparisons using mathematical language. Anytime you follow directions either to get somewhere or bust a move in dancing, you are thinking mathematically. Visual-spatial, visual-mechanical, or visual-kinesthetic learners already feel the math when they experience their own personal best records.

Chapter 10

Mathematics of Looking

The only thing worse than being blind is having sight but no vision.[1]
—Helen Keller

A visual explanation may be the missing piece when your child cries, "I just don't get it!" How can you help your child "get it" if you don't understand either? You have probably heard the phrase "seeing is believing," or heard stories about Missouri being nicknamed as "the show-me" state. Learning mathematics needs the "show-me" activities with actual eyesight so that the amazing mental eyesight "vision" of math relationships can appear.

As is true in most cases, just because *you* can "see" a math concept in a picture or diagram doesn't mean anyone else "sees" the same concept or the picture in the same way. Sometimes this "seeing the same thing differently" leads to creativity and sometimes it leads to misunderstanding. Several people can be looking at the same picture yet focus on different pieces. Fraction pictures can be especially frustrating when neither pair of eyes is wrong in their perception; each pair of eyes simply sees the same picture *differently*. Just ask Helen or Charles. The good news is that both pairs of eyes can learn *how to look*, a preferred option to screaming.

MATH RELATIONSHIPS AS SEEN THROUGH
A PHOTOGRAPHER'S EYES

"Learning to Look" was the title of a story in the *Boston Sunday Globe* (May 31, 1998) that described a photographer's trek through Acadia National Forest with a group of novice photographers to show them *how* to look, how to see with amazing vision through photography. The photographer explained and demonstrated how these new-look kinds of photographs would guarantee "brain engagement." The group learned how "to peel away the layers of pretty to find the engaging photograph underneath" through their own eyes.

Think for a minute about the mountains and lakes in Acadia National Forest, or about the mountains and lakes in the Shenandoah Valley, or about these in the Rocky Mountains. They are big, bigger than life at the right time of day. Mathematics is a system of relationships that can feel like a larger-than-life mountain of information. As new concepts with their related details are introduced in mathematics, it is easy to get overwhelmed with information and in so doing forget about the details of the overall math "story."

A good photograph includes the details that can tell the story behind the photographic image while still providing a glimpse of the larger view supporting the image. Your child can learn how to look at mathematics with the same amazing vision that a photographer uses to see a photograph and learn how to see an engaging "math photograph" that has enough details to tell a math story. Many design aspects of a good photograph also represent good brain-engaging mathematics. Balance, angle, shape, vanishing point proportion, and patterns of repetitions are all elements of a good photograph and of good mathematical thinking too.

BALANCE

Is there a balance of light and dark and a balance of foreground and background in the photograph? In mathematics, balance is everything. Balance between sides of an equation, balance between two symmetric sides of a shape, balance of weight between two objects, and balance of equivalent fractions and ratios are only a few of the balancing acts that your child must achieve in math and in photographs.

Hilary could complete most of the first grade math addition problems on the paper, but after a week, she might have only a few of the same problems correctly completed. For whatever reason, Hilary did not understand that the balance of the seesaw outside was the same idea of balance with the problems on the paper. A homemade wire coat hanger balance[2] helped Hilary understand the balance with objects, with mailing letters, and eventually with counting blocks of equal amounts. Her dad helped her make the number balance shown in Figure 10.1 so that she could now hang weights in the holes of the numbers and *see* the balance with numbers.

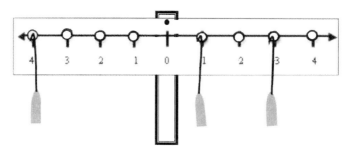

Figure 10.1   Hillary's dad's homemade balance.

ANGLE AND SHAPE

A diagonal line in a photograph gives the image a dynamic feel while a horizontal line yields a more stable image. Diagonal lines in shapes start in one corner and go to the opposite or nonadjacent corner and create all sorts of interesting angles. What if only the diagonals from *one* vertex of any polygon were allowed instead of showing all of the diagonals? The six polygons in Figure 10.2 show a few possibilities for how to see the dynamic of the diagonals as seen from one vertex. Are there any relationships between the number of diagonals from one vertex and the number of sides of the polygon? Do you see all of the triangles?

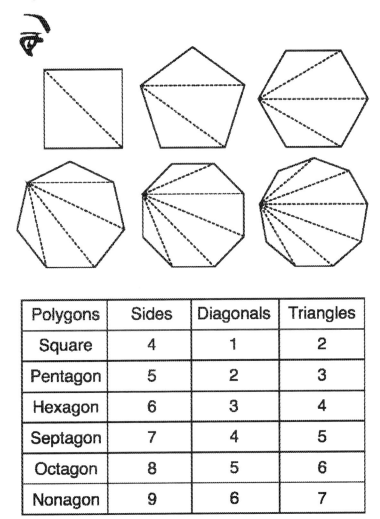

Polygons	Sides	Diagonals	Triangles
Square	4	1	2
Pentagon	5	2	3
Hexagon	6	3	4
Septagon	7	4	5
Octagon	8	5	6
Nonagon	9	6	7

Figure 10.2

VANISHING POINT PROPORTION

Good dynamic photographs will also have a vanishing point. Repeated shapes, like the sketched illustration of old-fashioned telephone poles in Figure 10.3, show an example of how a vanishing point is representative of the overlapping of similar shapes in math. The comparisons of the measures of these shapes are the numbers that would be in a proportion between two of the shapes. The triangles in the vanishing point image made by the poles are proportional. As the pole appears to shrink, the ground length to the vanishing point shrinks by the same multiple. Confirm these "details" of proportion with your calculator.

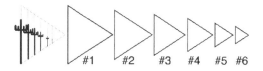

Similar Triangles			
	Pole height	Ground length	Ratio of pole height to ground length
Triangle #1	6	8	6/8
Triangle #2	5	6.66̄	5/6.66̄
Triangle #3	4	5.33̄	4/5.33̄
Triangle #4	3	4	3/4
Triangle #5	2	2.66̄	2/2.66̄
Triangle #6	1	1.33̄	1/1.33̄

Figure 10.3

PATTERNS OF REPETITION

An engaging photograph will have repeated patterns of shapes to echo the focus of the image. For example, the Acadia trekking photographer suggested that the foreground of a photograph of Bubble Rock should include some rounded rocks in order to echo the shape of Acadia's Bubble Rock in the background. Mathematics is also filled with repeating patterns to echo. One of those repeating math echoes appears in equivalent ratios. The proportional ratios in the similar triangles from the vanishing point have equivalent ratios and look very much like those decimal numbers in fifth grade equivalent ratios.

The larger picture of ratios can seem to be overwhelming to most middle-school students but not necessarily overwhelmingly beautiful. However, the good news is that both fractions and ratios "behave" the same way after they are written in symbols. In actuality, fractions *are* ratios, the specific kind of ratio that compares part pieces to whole amounts. Because these two ideas, fractions and ratios, share the same format, it is helpful to "free the notation" from the objects when trying to add or otherwise work with the notations. Use the objects to identify the item relationship and then let them go.

Skip counting also helps to recognize equivalent fractions—and ratios. Having the "whole picture" for the fraction (ratio) like the one for the 2/3 strip in Figure 10.4 makes the skip counting for equivalent fractions easier. The numerator of each equivalent fraction and ratio skip counts by 2 because it starts with 2 in the beginning. The denominator number skip counts by 3 also because the number 3 is in the first denominator.

$\frac{2}{3}$	$\frac{4}{6}$	$\frac{6}{9}$	$\frac{8}{12}$	$\frac{10}{15}$	$\frac{12}{18}$	$\frac{14}{21}$	$\frac{16}{24}$	$\frac{18}{27}$	$\frac{20}{30}$	$\frac{22}{33}$	$\frac{24}{36}$	

Figure 10.4 Fraction pattern strip.

BEN'S ENGAGING VIEW

Ben, a fifth grade student who started to play with different sizes of squares that might fit on the sides of triangles, identified some unexpected (to him) pattern repetitions. He was curious to see if he could discover any new patterns with the triangles after playing with some triangles from an activity in *Discover It.*[3] He also experimented with a computer sample sketch in *Geometer's Sketchpad.*[4] He did not know the Pythagorean Theorem first and then started out to prove it; he developed his own version of his "proof" through his experience and through his own "amazing eyes" investigation.

Ben started with several cutout squares, arranged them corner-to-corner to make triangles, and then used his calculator to record his data shown in Figure 10.5 to monitor the square areas that he could arrange to generate a right triangle. Some of those first triangles that he tried were not right triangles. Gradually, he honed in on which square areas he could use to make a right triangle. Continue reading about Ben's exploration and try to see the experience *through Ben's eyes.*

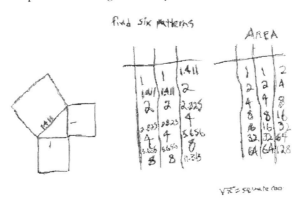

Figure 10.5 Ben's work.

During this exploration with triangles and squares, Ben figured out that putting together any three squares did not guarantee a right triangle when arranged corner-to-corner. His journal entry at this stage reflected his understanding of several patterns, but he still thought that the sides had to be doubled in order to make new right triangles. He was not yet aware that he had control of the side relationships. Eventually he developed the generality of the sides and squares that the books tell us is about the Pythagorean Theorem—and its converse.

Excerpt from Ben's journal entry: The purpose of this problem is to find all of the sides of a right triangle and see if there is a connection/pattern between sides of 3 squares which [*sic*] form the right triangle. To find these patterns you have to find the area and the sides of one set of squares which [*sic*] form a right triangle. The squares are also known as a, b and c. Here is an example that would work. Sq. a.= 1 sq. b = 1 and sq. c = 1.411. That is the sides of the squares.

KEEP IN MIND

Your child can learn how to look at math through a photographer's eyes and, like Hilary and Ben, begin to peel away the layers of "pretty" to find the engaging mathematics underneath. The beauty of the mathematics happens when your child starts to recognize their own ideas *within* the mathematics. When your child, like Ben, works on a new idea to uncover some new (to them) kind of relationships, then they are peeling away layers to find the engaging math underneath.

NOTES

1. http://www.brainyquote.com/quotes/quotes/h/helenkelle383771.html.
2. Apleman, *Everyday Math Activities*, 192.
3. Laycock, *Discover It* activity, http://www.activityresources.com/Discover-It.html.
4. *Geometer's Sketchpad*, http://www.dynamicgeometry.com/.

Chapter 11

Mathematics of Moving

A second cluster of spatial skills … involves the imagination and coordination in your mind of the infinite possibilities of lines of sight.[1] —John Dixon

Visual-spatial learners are acutely aware of the space around them: front, back, side, above, and below. If your child has a bent toward visual-spatial and visual-mechanical abilities and preferences, they may have already amazed you with their talents as dancers or sports players. What your child may not realize is that by participating in these activities, their bodies have already experienced some mathematical relationships.

Dance choreographers, like sports coaches, organize and manage space with their designs. The choreographer uses music tempo and the coach uses timing; both are functions of ratios. The musician and choreographer organize and manage movements with ratios of fast beats or slow beats, while the coach is managing movement in ratios of distance covered with speed and time. Neither one of these "designers" calculates these ratios with a paper and pencil or calculator. They know the feel. The dancers, players, and their respective "designers" know when these motions "feel" right, so their bodies already know the math.

Dance choreography requires attention to form in space with body positions of angles, balance, and control of the space on the stage. A dancer balances arm and leg positions while moving across the stage horizontally, diagonally, and vertically. Sports coaches must pay attention to angles of running directions in combination with speed and distance. Baseball home runs depend on the velocities of bats meeting balls at angles that ensure an out-of-the-ballpark distance and the runners must cover the 90-foot length between bases before the baseman touches the base. Dance is a sport form and game sports require a form of dance.

FEELING THE MATHEMATICS IN DANCE MOVEMENTS

Music and Dancing not only give great pleasure but have the honour of depending on Mathematics.[2] —Charles Sorel

Two of the many examples of body knowledge are in the choreography of individual dancers as well as in square dancing and other partner dancing. Both involve symmetric arrangements, balance, and diagonal moves. A dancer crosses the stage from the back stage left corner diagonally to front stage right corner and the square dancers cross partners with "do-si-do" moves. These diagonal physical moves are like the mathematics of the diagonals in the shapes shown in Figure 11.1 for polygons such as the rectangle, the isosceles trapezoid, and the regular pentagon.

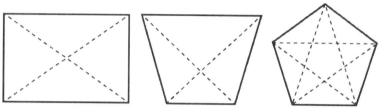

Figure 11.1

Because the pentagon diagonals generate a five-cornered star *and the star can be generated without lifting the pencil*, a Math Aficionado's or choreographer's question could be "Can other stars be drawn in other regular polygons in one continuous dance move and connect all of the dot points in the star?" Using the same size circle to inscribe all of the regular polygons will help keep the polygons limited in size and put boundaries on the shapes. Start with the regular inscribed pentagon like the one in Figure 11.2 to make marks on the circle's circumference that will locate the star points and then keep just the dots, the star, and the circle.

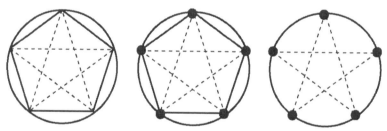

Figure 11.2

Remove the pentagon star from the circle and imagine adding another dot on the circle circumference. Make sure to keep equal distances on the circle circumference between the dots as in Figure 11.3. A math spelunker might ask about the number of dots, the number of points on a new star, and whether all the dots in the circles can make a star *without lifting the pencil*. They would start testing with easy examples like a regular hexagon and octagon. That round coffee filter can come in handy again by folding to find the hexagon and octagon star points. The inscribed hexagon and octagon will provide a visual guide for the dot locations.

Keep a record of the polygons, stars, and trials. Make a continuous star outline with the hexagon, skipping only one dot at a time. Next try skipping two dots. For the hexagon, a skip of one or two dots will not make a star that connects all of the dots. Draw another circle with eight equally spaced dots (with the help of an octagon and coffee filter) on the circle's circumference. The octagon will not make a star skipping only one dot, but it does make a star without lifting the pencil when skipping two dots.

Make your own stars with the septagon (seven points), the nonagon (nine points), and the decagon (ten points).

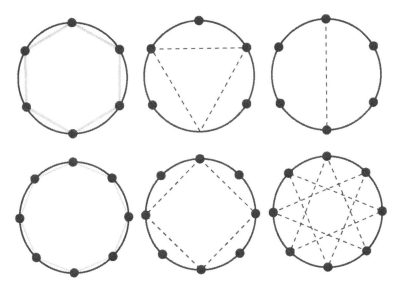

Regular Polygon Shapes for Stars								
	△	□	⬠	⬡	⬠	⯃	⯄	⬡
Number of sides	3	4	5	6	7	8	9	10
Skip one dot	no	no	yes	no		no		
Skip two dots	no	no	yes	no		yes		

Figure 11.3

This kind of activity releases the imagination to create divergent ideas for stars, polygons, and dance choreography. All of these stars will maintain symmetry with each turn of the star, making a very delightful dance arrangement. Patterns can seem to pop off the page from the records of all of their diagonals and polygons. New relationships can appear that may have nothing to do with the stars but have everything to do with discovering new relationships and connecting these new relationships to patterns. With this knowledge, a choreographer and your child can create some dynamic Star Aficionados!

THE BEAT OF PROPORTION

Why do certain notes and tones sound better when played together than others? Musicians and mathematicians make it so. The math is in the combinations of the ratios.

The musician knows complementary beats for songs and, for dance, the number of beats to a measure. The best example for these musically pleasant beats is in the whole, quarter, eighth note, and half note timing. Others fit in as well, but for this initial introduction, these are the notes that illustrate why good music sounds so pleasant to hear. The pleasantness is due to the math combinations of these ratios.

The whole note has a count of four in the whole measure but uses only one beat and the half note has a repeating count of two within the whole four-note count. The quarter note has four counts, one for each count in the whole measure. These ratios of counts begin to look a lot like those fractional ratios in the third or fourth grade homework papers. The relationship among the notes is shown in Figure 11.4. The eighth notes are double beats of the quarter notes, and the pattern continues to other notes.

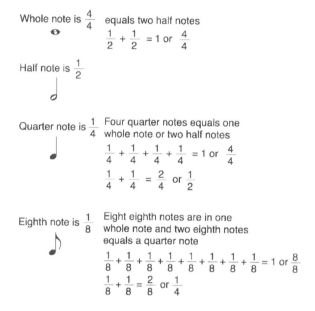

Figure 11.4

SPORTS ANGLES AND BASKETS

Take a moment to remember Menaechmus, the geometer who first described the parabola in the fourth century BC. He never made a layup, but he got game. —*Washington Post*, March 16, 2010

A difference of 10° for the angle that a baseball bat hits the ball can make the difference of a home run inside the park or outside the park. The batter knows how this feels. The basketball shooting guard can feel the correct angle for sinking the ball into the basket with a perfect parabolic curve. The billiard player knows the angles required to make the cue ball pocket the object ball. Hockey, football, and soccer players also have a sense for when and how to get the puck, football, and soccer ball, respectively, to their goal destinations.

Menaechmus' parabola is the reason basketballs go into the hoop from midcourt, three-point, free throw lines, or around the key. A golfer's driver will propel the ball in a high arc of that same parabola to make it go beyond 200 yards. A 20° angle hit of the baseball creates the right apex of the parabola vertex for the ball to go wide enough to leave the ballpark. A team or individual player that capitalizes on physics and Menaechmus cannot help but win!

The parabola that your child will see in an Algebra I or Algebra II class is the same parabola that lands the baseball into the Green Monster seats at Boston's Fenway Park. That parabola on a coordinate graph is a symmetric curve that has a maximum vertex at the top of the highest point before gravity makes it descend again. The equation for a sample parabola graph in Figure 11.5 has an equation $y = -x^2$ and is accompanied by a table of coordinate point locations, which represent all locations of the points on the parabola. The initial force of the hit, drive, or throw at one of those points will change the equation, the apex, and all the point locations.

There are three versions of the coordinate point parabola table in Figure 11.5 that represent the point values. In the first version, the square shape appears representing the x^2 and it changes in size as the number in the x column changes. The square area is now an abstraction (freed from the actual square area) because a side measure cannot be a negative integer. The second version shows the arithmetic and the third version shows the end result. The graph curve is controlled by the equation. The distance that the ball must travel for the home run also depends on the size of the field, horizontal and vertical velocity, and weather. It's a math event!

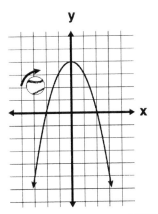

$y = -x^2$

x	y		x	y		x	y
-3	- ☐		-3	-(-3 • -3)		-3	-9
-2	- ☐		-2	-(-2 • -2)		-2	-4
-1	- ☐		-1	-(-1 • -1)		-1	-1
0			0	0 • 0		0	0
1	- ☐		1	-(1 • 1)		1	-1
2	- ☐		2	-(2 • 2)		2	-4
3	- ☐		3	-(3 • 3)		3	-9

Figure 11.5   Different parabola graph models.

SPORTS FIELDS AND ANGLES

The baseball diamond is 90 feet between bases so the hitter needs to run that distance fast and get to the base *before* the baseman can touch it with the ball. The professional basketball court is 94 feet long and the players know the best court positions for shooting the ball. The adult hockey field, soccer field, and football fields are all 120 yards long and players need to have the stamina and speed to outrun the opposing teams. All players have a feel for their best speed and timing. Each player in each sport knows the feel of the angle and the force needed to pass, hit, or throw to another team player. These are the muscle memories for angles, speed, and distance.

All of these fields and tables are rectangular and all require angle measures for optimum shooting, hitting, sinking, or passing. Let's play with some imaginary field dimensions and see what happens when the angle stays the same and only the sides of the rectangular field change. The four rectangles in Figure 11.6 have different length measures but the same width measure. A line indicated as an arrow starts from one of the corners at a 45° angle to the opposite side and continues in a diagonal manner back to the original side. Depending on the measurements of sides and angles, the line arrow will continue to "bounce" back and forth between sides.

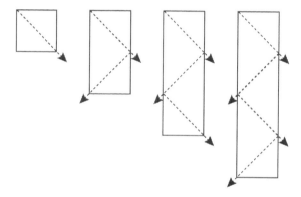

	Rectangles with constant width			
Width	1	1	1	1
Length	1	2	3	4
Number of arrows	1	2	3	4
Ratio of arrows to width	$\frac{1}{1}$	$\frac{2}{1}$	$\frac{3}{1}$	$\frac{4}{1}$
Ratio of arrows to length	$\frac{1}{1}$	$\frac{2}{2}$	$\frac{3}{3}$	$\frac{4}{4}$

Figure 11.6

Now, change the field dimensions using the same multiple on all sides. The first rectangle is a 1 × 1 rectangle. Multiply adjacent sides by the same multiple, keeping the same 45° angle. The examples in Figure 11.7 show the rectangles as squares with both sides doubled, tripled, etc. Again, compare the number of arrows with the widths and lengths of the squares using ratios. Another option for changing the field rectangle is to start with the 1 × 2 rectangle and then change its dimensions by the same multiple, this time using a multiple of two, three, and four for each new rectangle like the rectangles in Figure 11.8.

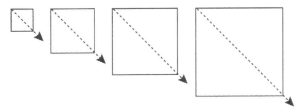

	Squares			
Width	1	2	3	4
Length	1	2	3	4
Number of arrows	1	1	1	1
Ratio of arrows to width	$\frac{1}{1}$	$\frac{1}{2}$	$\frac{1}{3}$	$\frac{1}{4}$
Ratio of arrows to length	$\frac{1}{1}$	$\frac{1}{2}$	$\frac{1}{3}$	$\frac{1}{4}$

Figure 11.7

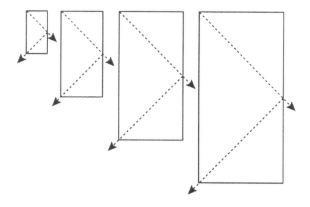

	Rectangles			
Width	1	2	3	4
Length	2	4	6·	8
Number of arrows	2	2	2	2
Ratio of arrows to width	$\frac{2}{1}$	$\frac{2}{2}$	$\frac{2}{3}$	$\frac{2}{4}$
Ratio of arrows to length	$\frac{2}{2}$	$\frac{2}{4}$	$\frac{2}{6}$	$\frac{2}{8}$

Figure 11.8

The size and the dimensions of sports fields may change according to age groups, but the fields are all optimum for playing the game. The field designers may have originally tested different-sized fields, even with ratio dimensions such as a 1 × 2 rectangle like the ones in Figure 11.9. The first 1 × 2 rectangle width was doubled, tripled, and quadrupled, but the length was changed by a different factor. The second rectangle length is 1.5 times the first rectangle length. The third rectangle has a length that is double the first. What happened for the fourth rectangle length?[3] How did these changes affect the number of "bounces"?

The arrows on these rectangles may eventually be symbols for vectors representing the force required for the players to zigzag or they may indicate the direction of the cue ball to pocket the object ball on a rectangular pool table. These examples with rectangles and their changing dimensions provide a playing field for you and your child to investigate and play with ratios, angles, and changes in shape dimensions.

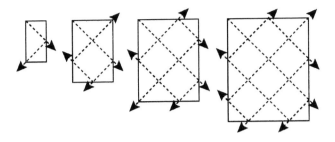

	Rectangles			
Width	1	2	3	4
Length	2	3	4	5
Number of arrows	2	4	6	8
Ratio of arrows to width	$\frac{2}{1}$	$\frac{4}{2}$	$\frac{6}{3}$	$\frac{8}{4}$
Ratio of arrows to length	$\frac{2}{2}$	$\frac{4}{3}$	$\frac{6}{4}$	$\frac{8}{5}$

Figure 11.9

KEEP IN MIND

Mathematics is the communicator, the language behind the description for personal best performances, teamwork design, and efficient direction. In sports the best and most effective movements through space are known first by the body and then measured with the mathematics. The physics of each move describes what is happening to make the body feel those most effective and efficient body movements.

NOTES

1. Dixon, *The Spatial Child*, 34.
2. http://www.goodreads.com/quotes/482132-music-and-dancing-not-only-give-great-pleasure-but-have.
3. Answer: The first rectangle length was multiplied by 2.5 to get the fourth rectangle length.

Chapter 12

Mathematics of Building

Ah, to build, to build! That is the noblest art of all the arts.[1] —Henry Wadsworth Longfellow

Young Frankie's mom gave her nine-year-old son a set of Froebel blocks, and just a decade or so later, when he was 22, Frank Lloyd Wright designed his first building, one of many in an outstanding architectural career. While Wright was designing buildings and homes, Bucky's mom enrolled him in a Froebelian kindergarten in Massachusetts. This young man grew up to be Buckminster Fuller, the developer of the geodesic dome (like the one at Epcot Center). Both men were influenced early in their lives by the shape arrangements, form design, and assembly of shapes in mathematics.

Early stories of Buckminster Fuller sound like current stories of curious young minds—possibly your child, too. Fuller's biography tells of how young Bucky brought things home from his explorations in some nearby woods to create new items that could push, pull, or turn things. However, as he grew older, he had difficulty with formal geometry because his "push pull" visual-mechanical mental thinking could not embrace the mathematical abstraction of a zero-dimensional dot. It is a good thing that he got over this premature precision experience!

"My child builds all sorts of things but cannot understand math" is the lament of one parent who is trying to encourage their child in math despite their child's low school grades. This comment is familiar to parents, especially when their children are talented visual-mechanical learners who do not use their hands-on ability in math class. The child as builder already mentally sees the shape and proportion concepts and just needs the symbols to express them. Most of the building toys have the mathematics incorporated into the designs for this noblest of art forms. It begins with math measurements, counting, comparing, and relationships.

Froebel Gifts block sets, Lego blocks, Magformer shapes, Polydrons, and K'NEX sets are commercial versions of sanded-down leftover lumber scraps, straws, pipe cleaners, cardboard boxes, and sticks from nearby woods. The mathematics is in the building, the artful assembly, and in the relationships of balance and equivalences. The construction details and limitations faced by architects and construction contractors start early with young ideas of shape form, block size comparisons, and angle measures.

BUILDING BLOCKS FOR SHAPE FORM

Architects build scale models of buildings before the construction contractor even picks up the hammer. Your child builds small cities, castles, and model machinery. The building toys are already child-sized so the scale is already built into the models. Older children can fold pieces of paper to make the smaller-scaled models of larger buildings. In math classes, these paper-folding shapes are called "nets" for learning about volume and surface area in fifth grade or generating formulas in algebra.

Polyhedra nets are flat, two-dimensional, straight-sided versions of shapes that fold up into three-dimensional forms, similar to the post office flat boxes that fold up to mail things in. An architect's three-dimensional net will likely have a roof angle, but the beginning three-dimensional shapes will most likely resemble the shoe box, the post office box, or the cylinder in Figure 12.1 that folds up to make a building model. Cylinder nets fold up from flat surfaces to represent towers, turrets, or silos. Because the cylinder has a round base, it is considered a three-dimensional solid rather than a polyhedra net, since a polyhedral net has only straight edges.

Figure 12.1   Three-dimensional nets.

The mathematics of making one of these nets can begin as early as your child wants to fit shapes together. The net is created when your child's two-dimensional "sides" shape fold up to form an enclosed three-dimensional shape. Polydrons link together and Magformers magnetically connect for different sizes and shapes of geometric nets. Your child's creative imagination can invent their own shapes on paper so that they can cut out, assemble, and fold to make their own models and designs.

RATIOS FOR STAIRS

The ratio of risers to treads in steps is dictated by a building code so that people do not trip while going up or down the stairs. That code limits the risers to be between seven inches and four inches and requires a minimum of eleven inches for the tread. Different states have different building codes and regulations vary for inside stairs and outside stairs. For the math example in Figure 12.2, the four-stair-step slope ratio will use a seven riser to an eleven-tread ratio. The math of this stair-step ratio is a topic in any first-year algebra class; the slope ratio in a linear equation.

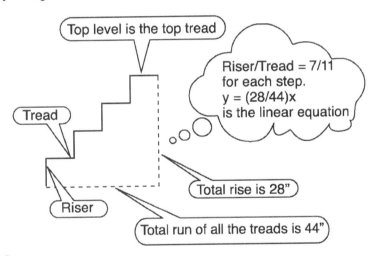

Figure 12.2

The total riser measure for these four steps is 4 × 7 or twenty-eight inches between floor levels. The distance that these four steps must cover is 4 × 11 from the first step up to top level (including the top floor level) for a forty-four-inch total measure. In an algebra class, these totals are also used as an expression for the overall slope ratio. In the fourth grade, your child learned how to calculate equivalent fractions. Later, you child learned about equivalent ratios. The ratio between one riser and one tread 7/11 compares with the equivalent ratio 28/44 from the totals. The code applies to the single riser and tread; the architect and the carpenter need the total distance equivalent ratio.

A change in the total rise distance will change the slope and the number of steps. Carpenters tend to use whole inches unless a fractional inch will give them a better arrangement and cut. Also, carpenters know that they need to allow for an adjustment to the measurements due to sawdust loss caused by the cut. The graph of the slope relationship and the carpenter's problem in Figure 12.3 shows up in an algebra class as a line on a coordinate axis.

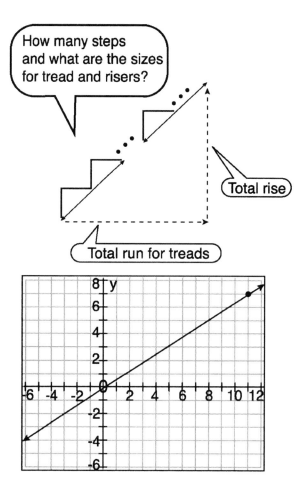

Figure 12.3

ROOF PITCH, RATIOS, AND ANGLES

A roof is supported by several rafters; the number and length of the rafters depend on the width of the building and the pitch of the roof. The pitch of the roof is controlled by the angle generated by a ratio between the height of the roof at its peak and one-half of the width of the building. The shape of that one-half of the roof shape going from roof eave to center rafter and following the roof edge is a right triangle. These right triangle and ratios appear in many grades: in a high-school trig class, in fourth grade as equivalent fractions, and in eighth grade or middle school when studying similar triangles and the Pythagorean Theorem relationship.

In a trig class, the tangent ratio of the roof pitch angle is calculated by sine ratio (the rafter height opposite the angle compared with roof line) over cosine ratio (the width part of the house adjacent to the angle compared with roof line). The tangent ratio is associated with slope or pitch of the roof because it *is* the name for the ratio of the sine to cosine. That tangent ratio is also the riser-to-tread ratio used for the stairs. All three triangles in Figure 12.4 share the same diagram showing the roof, rafters, and the angle pitch; the trig ratios for the rafters; and the similar right triangles made by the rafters and roof (or risers and treads or telephone poles).

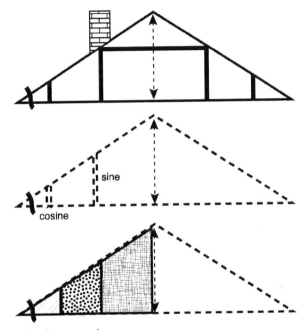

Figure 12.4   Three triangle connections.

A PYTHAGOREAN TUNNEL

Building the ancient tunnel in Samos, like constructing stairs and roofs and creating vanishing points, required that the Greek surveyors use similar triangles and ratios. The tunnel of Samos, sometimes called the tunnel of Eupalinos, was measured and dug in the sixth century BC without cranes or modern-day instruments. The city planners of Samos needed water from the other side of the mountain so they decided to dig the 4,000 feet *through* the mountain, instead of going around it. Jeff and Mike, two middle-school "math surveyors," built a model of that mountain shown in Figure 12.5 and described the mathematics behind the tunnel building efforts.

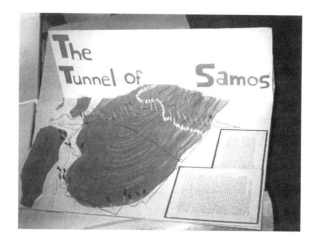

Figure 12.5

KEEP IN MIND

Whether your child builds scale models of buildings with nets, constructs stairs, measures a roof, or uses paper maché models of mountains, their hands are involved in the noblest art form while their minds are engaged in the mathematics. Froebel, Wright, Fuller, those ancient Greek surveyors, and your child have amazing eyes that can "see" new ideas and new arrangements to build with the noblest art using mathematics.

NOTE

1. http://quotationsbook.com/quote/2852/.

Conclusion

What Can Parents Do?

Parents find themselves unofficially involved in a similar dilemma. They want to help their children with mathematics but they fear that little good will come of the blind leading the blind.[1] —W. W. Sawyer

By the time your child enters school, you have served as their growth curator, lead teacher, and chief inspiration officer. You helped them learn the basics of an entire language, maybe two or more. Your child has learned to walk and find things under your watch. They have learned to play with others and learned some rules about behavior. Your child has probably learned to say the counting words and hopefully knows that each word names a different amount of items. You should be amazed at what you have helped your child to achieve. In school, it is time for your child to learn more about languages, and one of them is the language of math.

If you are a Math Aficionado parent, you need to be honest with yourself about how you felt on those first few days in that advanced math class when the math symbols felt like Taser shocks to your math confidence. Your child's early addition problems like 3 + 4 or the algebra equations that look like $y = x^2 + 4x + 4$ may seem easy to you now but can be Tasers for them. Remembering your own Taser shocks can make you a better champion for your child as they decipher the meanings behind the symbols in *their* classes now. Your job is not to "fix" your child; your job is to team with them to help them build their Taser-free math self-confidence.

If you are a Math Avoider parent, you also need to be honest with yourself and your child about how *you* felt on those unhappy days in your math classes when possibly every day felt like a Taser day, but *not* from the it-never-made-sense-to-me-so-you-have-a-ticket-to-not-try perspective. If your child is headed down that Math Avoider road, it will help them more if you empathize, acknowledge their feelings, and then partner with them and be willing to learn and explore together. What happened to make you a Math Avoider is not as important to your child as what the two of you can do together to avoid repeating those experiences.

Expand your parietal lobe to encompass your own neural "parental lobe" to encourage your child to perceive mathematics in *their personal* way. Don't put your child through what you had to endure; share what you did enjoy. One very concerned parent

125

was refreshingly honest when he admitted that he had been required to memorize the math facts, so he thought he was supposed to require it of his own child. He acknowledged that it wasn't working and that his insistence was driving a wedge in their father-daughter relationship. Interestingly, both father and daughter were very good with mathematical thinking, just in different ways.

How can the blind lead the blind? Sometimes the Math Avoider leaders are more helpful than the Math Aficionado leaders. The Avoiders know what it feels like to feel the shame and frustration associated with memories of anxiety in mathematics classes, so they are unlikely to minimize the pain, or worse, tell the child to "get over it." They can, however, compound the problem by offering such victim-oriented comments as "I hated math, too." These kinds of comments are not helpful because they do not provide any sense of empowerment or guidance about how to *think* about the math.

You can't do it all, but you *can* ask questions to engage your child's thinking, *before* the wailing starts. The best way to reduce emotional wailing is to redirect attention toward a more focused direction using a few questions that require thinking and opinions, *especially* opinions. Respond to feelings behind the wailing first and *then* ask some clever questions about the math using a topic that your child already likes. The distraction can be simple or complex, depending on your child's likes and dislikes. Let your child teach you how they think. You don't have to *do* anything but listen.

Homework problems usually include practice problems from the day's math lesson. Practice works for shooting baskets but is not very helpful for *understanding* math, especially if your child does not understand the concept. One good place to start talking about the concept is to ask some questions about what the specific math topic reminds them of. Your child's own metaphors and analogies work best. You are not supposed to replace the teacher, but you *can* enhance and individualize the teacher's work. Ask questions, use metaphors, and listen to your child's perceptions. Remember, the questions do not have to have immediate answers!

Do some math spelunking with your child through questions and other lateral thinking, creative, and imagination-provoking strategies. Ask questions about comparing things. Let them tell stories about the math topics like the stories in the *Number Devil* book. If your child has already passed "Go" and gone straight to Math Avoider Jail, then your task is more difficult from a psychological perspective, but not impossible. Do *not* ask questions like "Why don't you get it?" If they knew that, then there wouldn't be a problem. Do ask questions like "What was the last thing you did like or understand about _____?" Spelunk the math with their preferences.

The visual-spatial learner is a whole-to-part learner who tends to learn complex ideas easily but struggles with details. They do *not* learn by drill and repetition.[2] Some tactics that can help visual-spatial learners are color-coding, brainstorming webs, and completing graphic organizers by organizing the material *their* way first, using math tools of carpentry, drafting, or cooking, and other ideas shared earlier in this book. Remember, do not do anything that your child can do or can learn how to do. As a kindergarten teacher once said, "I already know how to cut with scissors. My children need to learn the skill no matter what it looks like."

COLOR-CODING

For GPS directions or any visual directing focus, use color-coding and let your child select colors to guide line of sight or color-code categories. Your child can select their preferred colors to highlight specific directions such as red for left-to-right, green for around, and blue for diagonal. If *they* choose the colors, then *they* are more involved in the process and that color dislike, like kindergartner Anne had for green, is avoided! If your child is already "passived-out" and a front-and-center Math Avoider, then even choosing colors for a math problem is threatening. They will be afraid that they will choose the *wrong* colors.

It isn't the color; it is the fear, the *irrational* fear. The reasoning: they have been wrong so many times in math already, why would this be any different? Just to be able to select their colors gets them involved at the beginning stage of *possessing* the problem, a precursor to taking control of their own learning. Each stage is a big step. Now let them assign one color to a place value category digit: one color for hundreds, another color for tens, and the last color for the ones units. They can even color-code multiplication problems like Jamie's fourth grade problem in Figure C.1. Use colors in any way that helps them understand.

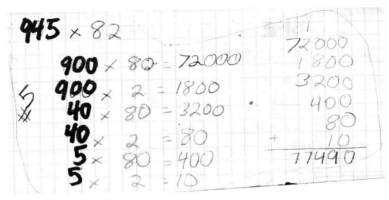

Figure C.1   Jamie's color-coding.

BRAINSTORMING WEBS AND OTHER ORGANIZERS

Brainstorming webs like Miguel's in Figure C.2 have a circle in the center of the page that includes the name of the math concept or topic. Lines radiate out from that circle with all related ideas that your child can imagine. No judgments; all adjustments happen later. Miguel's web has spokes with several versions of the Pythagorean Theorem. The explanations of these formulas include similar shapes (squares, pentagons, semicircles) and are written around the edges of the web diagram. Other spokes have the Law of Cosines. Miguel's fascination with the Pythagorean relationship began in middle school and has continued into high school.

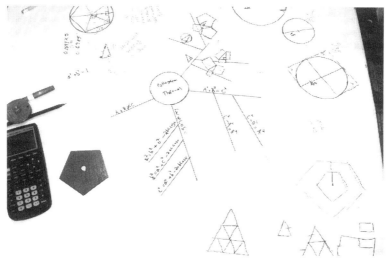

Figure C.2   Miguel's brainstorm web.

Graphic organizers like Judy's fourth grade version of "Fraction" in Figure C.3 can also help your child with organizational thinking. When your child is making decisions about completing the organizer, they must be in a judgment-free zone. Just the *process* of completing the organizer generates opinions and conversation about the math topic; opinions cannot be "wrong." You can partner with your child to share opinions, but any requirement that your child think like you is asking for a speedier trip to Math Avoider-dom. Any tactic that requires some decision-making by your child contributes to their thinking deeper about a concept.

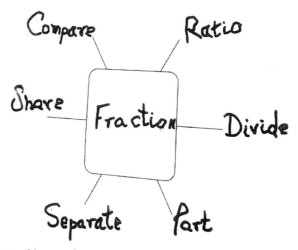

Figure C.3   Judy's graphic organizer.

USE THE TOOLS OF MATH

Young children can use string pulled tight with a piece of chalk to draw circles and their older siblings can use a compass to draw circles. Several other examples of homemade measuring and drafting tools are described in *Exploring Everyday Math* such as the wire coat hanger balance[3] in Figure C.4. If you and your visual-mechanical child make the coat hanger balance, don't be surprised if they are better at it than you are. A coat hanger balance, a string compass, or a T-square can help your child, and Hilary, because a hands-on activity provides the opportunity for the mental organization behind understanding.

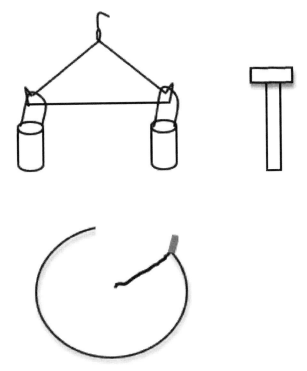

Figure C.4

TOP FIVE DO LIST

1. Encourage your child to use numbers whenever the opportunity arises: money, miles, quarts, ounces, feet, angles, circumference, areas, perimeters, and others. This suggestion means letting your child do the measuring, counting, making change, and pouring while you watch. Talk about what is happening and why it is happening. Saying the words for the numbers does not mean that the child can count correctly; it means that the child can say the words and is learning to enunciate the words like any child would first learn to say a word.

2. Try to find at least three solutions or methods to every math problem. Your child can write the word problem or calculation problem on a 5 × 8 index card and post

it on the refrigerator or other public family display location. For the next week, or few days, every family member writes a different solution, method, or "answer" on different 5 × 8 cards. All suggested solutions are welcomed. At the end of the designated period, schedule a time for everyone to gather to talk about their cards, both the similarities and the differences. Another activity is to play an *Answer Game*: post the answer on the refrigerator and solicit child-created problems to match.

To make a word problem activity more interesting, write each sentence from several word problems on separate cards, put the sentence cards in a bag, and let children pick a sentence (without looking) from the bag to try to put together a word problem that makes sense. If the sentences do not make sense, that is okay; just draw another card until the situation has enough information to solve. Put the cards back into the bag at the end of the activity so that they can be available for another problem activity. Not only does your child learn what is "enough" information to make a problem, but they also learn how to generate a math story.

3. Accept mistakes. Yes, you read this correctly. Accept mistakes and capitalize on them by asking about the thinking behind them. Encourage your child to talk about their thinking and be careful to *not* sound punitive. As a famous mathematician Henri Poincaré said, "How is an error possible in mathematics?"[4] To understand what Poincaré is really saying is to understand real mathematical exploration. Give your child the gift of learning about what to do *after* they make a mistake and talk about how making mistakes can give them new information. Both George Pólya and Henri Poincaré valued mistakes; each expressed this value in his own way.

4. Trust your child. Allow them to explain their reasoning to you. Even though it may not make sense to you right away, it does make sense to them from their perspective. Continue to allow them to talk so that eventually it does make some sort of sense to you. Besides, you may learn some mathematics that you had never thought of before! You will learn how they see a problem and its solution, and it will probably be significantly different from the way you see it.

   Both of you can use the "why" question as you endeavor to understand what each of you is trying to say. If at first you do not understand what your child is saying, that's okay. Keep asking for honest clarification, but stop before you become the interrogator. "I don't know [why], but it still works," was Hayden's fourth grade initial response before he learned how to talk about his thinking. Children do not need to feel that they are on trial for growing up. The objective is to show them *how to express* their mathematical thinking in a safe place.

5. Be willing to learn along with your child rather than require of yourself that you learn it first. You can miss out on some delightful experiences if you require that you know the outcome beforehand. The Mathematical Sciences Education Board Report *Everybody Counts* cautions us that no one can really teach mathematics[5] but notes that we can stimulate students to learn by allowing them to examine, explore, apply, and communicate mathematics.

KEEP IN MIND

Some Math Aficionado parents, in their enthusiasm to plant their love of mathematics into their child's mental garden, tend to backhoe the farm instead of tilling the soil. The result is a math-anxious student in the making. The Math Avoider parents, in their efforts to make their child feel better about being frustrated, tend to empathize to the point of disempowerment. Neither is very helpful. Use any strategies that encourage your child's learning preferences so that they feel that they have a chance at learning about the math relationships. Answer *their* questions and not what you *think* should be their questions. Take turns and partner with your child.

Now that you have new insight into mathematics and, possibly, some new insights into how you and your child view mathematics, let your imagination light up your math life! During this Math Homework Adventure, you saw some new ideas and were reminded of some familiar ones from a different perspective. Use your billions of neurons to expand on the visualization, lateral thinking, and "perceiving" insight squeezed into these pages to see mathematics differently. Now it is your turn to let your child show you how to help them with a different math repertoire using their thinking and their language. You can translate later. Happy spelunking!

NOTES

1. Sawyer, *Vision in Elementary Mathematics*, 1.
2. Silverman, *Identifying Visual-Spatial and Auditory-Sequential Learners*, 23.
3. Apleman, *Exploring Everyday Math*, 192.
4. Poincaré, *Braineyquotes.com*.
5. *Everybody Counts*, 50.

Glossary

This glossary is generated by definitions provided by students. Please refer to a mathematical dictionary for formal mathematical definitions.

additive inverse—zero, the "subtraction" to get to zero

algorithm—operation or procedure with numbers—add, subtract, multiply, divide, and all the other defined procedures

area—coverage inside of a shape

auditory-sequential—learns best by hearing step-by-step directions

circumference—the length around a circle space

circumscribed—when a polygon's corners touch the circumference of a circle

commutative—the name given to the situation when the operation works both ways

composition—building a term or shape with component pieces

congruent—the name assigned to shapes when their number measures are equal

coordinate points—a pair of numbers that shows where two number directions meet

cosine—the shift of a sine curve; the ratio of adjacent side to hypotenuse side in a right triangle.

cylinder—a three-dimensional tube-looking shape

decomposition—taking apart a term or a shape into component parts

diagonal—the one-dimensional line that connects two corners in a polygon

diameter—the one-dimensional line that connects the opposite ends on a circle circumference through the center

digits—0, 1, 2, 3, 4, 5, 6, 7, 8, 9

directional reading—how your eyes track while reading something

exponents—the small number in the upper right side of a term that tells how many times that term is multiplied by itself

factor—decomposing by only using division. No fractions.

Fractions—part-of-it as compared to all-of-it ratio

imaginary number—a number that does not belong to the Real number set

inscribed—when a polygon is inside of a circle and the vertices of the polygon touch the circle's circumference integer—a whole number that has either a + or a "−" indicator. No fractions.

inverse operation—the opposite operation that takes numbers back to their "origin." For addition, the origin is 0; for multiplication, the origin is 1.

isosceles—the adjective assigned to a triangle or quadrilateral when the two opposite sides are congruent

Lattice method—an algorithm developed by John Napier

lightsaber—the long stretch of light in Star Wars and the name given to single long strips of numbers

logarithm—how to write a number that equals the exponent

parabola—a curve that is symmetric and has an equation with the highest exponent of 2, like $y = x^2$

parallel—two lines or line segments that will never touch

parallelogram—a quadrilateral with opposite parallel sides

perimeter—the line distance around the boundary of a shape

perpendicular—when a vertical line crosses a horizontal line

polygon—straight-sided two-dimensional shapes

polyhedra—straight-sided three-dimensional shapes

prism—many-sided polyhedra

quadrilateral—four-sided polygon

radius—half of a diameter

regular—the adjective for all sides having equal measures and all angles are equal to each other

rhombus—a quadrilateral with all adjacent sides congruent but not necessarily a square

similarity—same shape with proportional sides

sine—a continuous curve in trig; the curve goes through the origin (0, 0) and is the ratio between the opposite side and the hypotenuse in a right triangle

slope of a line—the ratio used as a coefficient to x in a linear equation; the ratio tells how high the line rises on y in relation to the run on the x axis between two points on the same line

square numbers—when a number of items can be arranged into a square

symmetry—when two sides of a shape exactly match

tangent—a noncontinuous curve in trig; the curve goes through the origin (0, 0) and is defined by the ratio of the sine over the cosine ratios of the sides of a right triangle

trapezoid—a quadrilateral that has exactly two parallel sides

trigonometry—a kind of math that studies the ratios of sides in a right triangle that match to angles

vertex—a corner of a polygon or polyhedra

visual-spatial—learns best through visual and context methods

volume—what fills up the contents of a three-dimensional shape

References

Abbott, Edwin A. *Flatland*. New York: Penguin Books, 1884.

Alsina, Claudi, and Roger B. Nelson. *Math Made Visual*. Washington, DC: The Mathematical Association of America, 2006.

Apleman, Maja, and Julie King. *Exploring Everyday Math*. Portsmouth: Heinemann Publications, 1993.

Armstrong, Thomas. *Multiple Intelligences in the Classroom*. Alexandria: Association for Supervision and Curriculum Development, 1994.

Bennett, Dan. *Pythagoras Plugged In*. Emeryville: Key Curriculum Press, 2003.

Bowden, Edward M., and Jung-Beeman, Mark. "Aha! Insight experience correlates with solution activation in the right hemisphere." *Psychonomic Bulletin & Review* 10 (September 2003): 730–37.

Brosterman, Norman. *Inventing Kindergarten*. New York: Harry N. Abrams, 1997.

Burns, Marilyn. *Math: Facing an American Phobia*. Sausalito: Math Solutions Publications, 1998.

Carroll, Lewis (Charles Dodgson). *Alice's Adventures in Wonderland*. New York: Macmillan, 1865.

Courant, Richard, and Herbert Robbins. *What Is Mathematics?* Rev. Ian Stewart. Oxford: Oxford University Press, 1996. https://yakovenko.files.wordpress.com/2009/11/cr.pdf.

Davis, Philip J., and Reuben Hersh. *The Mathematical Experience*. Boston: Houghton-Mifflin Company, 1981.

De Bono, Edward. *New Think*. New York: Avon Publishers, 1968.

Dixon, John Philo, Ph.D. *The Spatial Child*. Springfield: Charles C. Thomas, 1983.

Dominguez, Manuel, and Mary Laycock. *Discover It*. Hayward: Activity Resources, 1986.

Draper, Catheryne. *The Algebra Game: Linear Graphs, Quadratic Equations, Conic Sections, and Trig Functions*. Rowley: Didax Education Inc., 2016.

Dunn, Rita, and Kenneth Dunn. *Teaching Students Through Their Individual Learning Styles*. Reston: Reston Publishing Company, 1978.

Enzensberger, Hans Magnus. *The Number Devil: A Mathematical Adventure*. New York: Metropolitan Books, 1997.

Gardner, Howard. *The Unschooled Mind*. New York: BasicBooks, 2011.

Geometer's Sketchpad 4.0. Emeryville: Key Curriculum Press, 2001. Accessed May 26, 2016, http://www.dynamicgeometry.com/.

Grandin, Temple. *Thinking In Pictures*. New York: Vintage Books, 2006. http://www.grandin. com/inc/visual.thinking.html.

Gregorc, Anthony F. *An Adult's Guide to Styles*. Columbia: Gregorc Associates, Inc., 1986.

Hersh, Reuben, and Vera John-Steiner. *Loving + Hating Mathematics*. Princeton: Princeton University Press, 2011.

Hilton, Peter, and Jean Pedersen. *Fear No More: An Adult Approach to Mathematics*. Menlo Park: Addison Wesley Publishing Company, 1983.

Irwin-De Vitis, Linda, Karen Bromley, and Marcia Modlo. *50 Graphic Organizers for Reading, Writing, and More*. New York: Scholastic Professional Books, 1999.

"In Basketball, Shooting Angle Has a Big Effect on the Chances of Scoring." *Washington Post*, March 16, 2010, http://www.washingtonpost.com/wp-dyn/content/article/2010/03/15/ AR2010031502017.html.

Jacobs, Harold R. *Mathematics: A Human Endeavor*. New York: W. H. Freeman and Company, 1982.

Johnson, Spencer. *Who Moved My Cheese?* New York: G. P. Putnam's Sons, 1998.

King, Julie. "The Power to Make Predictions." *Connects Magazine* (January, February 2007): 8–10.

Kolpas, Sidney J. *The Pythagorean Theorem: Eight Classic Proofs*. Palo Alto: Dale Seymour Publications, 1992.

Lavoie, Richard. *How Difficult Can This Be?* Accessed May, 22, 2016, https://www.youtube. com/watch?v=zHQA3u-KPXc.

Lubinski, David. "Spatial Ability and STEM." *Personality and Individual Differences* 49 (2010): 344–51. https://my.vanderbilt.edu/smpy/files/2013/02/Lubinski_2010_spatial.pdf.

Marolda, Maria R., and Patricia S. Davidson. "Assessing Mathematical Abilities and Learning Approaches." *Windows of Opportunity*. Reston: National Council of Teachers of Mathematics, 1994.

National Council of Teachers of Mathematics (NCTM). *Principles and Standards for School Mathematics*. Reston, VA: The Council, 2000.

National Research Council. *Everybody Counts*. 1989. http://www.mathcurriculumcenter.org/ PDFS/CCM/summaries/everybody_counts_summary.pdf.

Ornstein, Robert. *The Right Mind: Making Sense of the Hemispheres*. New York: Harcourt Brace and Company, 1997.

Osborn, Alex. *Your Creative Power: How to Use Imagination*. New York: Charles Scribner's Sons, 1949.

Park, Gregory, David Lubinski, and Camilla P. Benbow. "Recognizing Spatial Intelligence." *Scientific American* (November 2010). http://www.scientificamerican.com/article/ recognizing-spatial-intel/.

Smith, Sanderson M. *Agnesi to Zeno*. Emeryville: Key Curriculum Press, 1996.

Sawyer, W. W. *Vision in Elementary Mathematics*. Baltimore: Pelican Books, 1964.

Sawyer, W. W. *Mathematician's Delight*. Baltimore: Pelican Books, 1943.

Shah, Priti, and Akira Miyake, ed. *Cambridge Handbook of Visuospatial Thinking*. Cambridge, England: Cambridge University Press, 2005.

Silverman, Linda Kreger. *Upside Down Brilliance—Strategies for Teaching Visual-Spatial Learners*. Denver: DeLeon Publishing, 2002.

Silverman, Linda Kreger. "Identifying Visual-Spatial and Auditory-Sequential Learners: A Validation Study." http://visualspatial.org/files/idvsls.pdf.

Sword, Lesley K. "I Think in Pictures, You Teach in Words." The Gifted Visual Spatial Learner, 2000.

Tierney, Cornelia. "Patterns in the Multiplication Table." *The Arithmetic Teacher* 32 (March 1985): 36–40.

Tobias, Sheila. *Overcoming Math Anxiety*. Boston: Houghton Mifflin Company, 1978.

Turnbull, H. W. *The Great Mathematicians*. New York: Barnes and Noble, 1993.

Vail, Priscilla L. *Learning Styles*. Rosemont: Modern Learning Press, 1992.

Von Oech, Roger. *A Whack on the Side of the Head*. New York: Warner Books, 1983.

West, Thomas G. *In The Mind's Eye*. Amherst: Prometheus Press, 2009.

West, Thomas G. *Thinking Like Einstein*. Amherst: Prometheus Press, 2004.

Whitin, David J. "Becca's Investigation." *The Arithmetic Teacher* (October 1993): 78–81.

MATERIALS

Algebra Game: Linear Graphs, Quadratic Equations, Conic Sections, and Trig Functions

AngLegs

Creativity

Chips or disks

Coffee filters (round)

Discover It

Froebel's Gifts

Geometry Sketchpad

Grid paper

Imagination

Linking cubes

Magformers

Markers—colors

Polydrons

Parquetry Design Blocks

Patty Paper AKA Tracing paper

Socks and container for Sock Box

Unifix cubes

Visualization

Wire coat hangers

Yarn

About the Author

Catheryne Draper's tenure in math education has crossed the half-century mark. Draper started as a high-school teacher and then served as a district supervisor, state-level advisor, professional development consultant, and math coach/teacher for both large urban and smaller public and private schools. She has taught math at all levels of kindergarten through college classrooms in addition to maintaining for almost 35 years an ongoing practice working with individual children and adults who "see" mathematics differently.

She has worked as a math editor for textbook and supplementary materials in regular education and special education. She opened the Math Studio in the early 1980s to pursue her passion of providing visual and tactile instruction for all students. Her 25-plus-year tenure working with clients of the Massachusetts Rehabilitation Commission brought predictably successful results as she helped them succeed in their math learning goals.

Draper developed and published *The Algebra Game Program*, an instructional and assessment card program for classrooms and individuals. In addition to teaching and working in educational publishing, Draper has also written articles for and contributed to many journal publications about mathematics education pedagogy.

Draper graduated with a B.S. in mathematics and an M.Ed. degree in mathematics education and supervision from the University of Georgia. While in Georgia, she was instrumental in developing a K–8 instructional and assessment tool with a computer-driven assessment component and was responsible for bringing computer terminals into the district's high-school curriculum, predating today's technology involvement by decades. After leaving Georgia, Draper worked with national assessment companies and publishing companies prior to opening the doors of the Math Studio to further usher in positive changes in mathematics education.

CPSIA information can be obtained
at www.ICGtesting.com
Printed in the USA
BVOW02*1917071216
469967BV00006B/9/P